THE GODDESS DICTIONARY

of

WORDS AND PHRASES

⚛ THE LOCHLAINN SEABROOK COLLECTION ⚛

AMERICAN CIVIL WAR
Abraham Lincoln Was a Liberal, Jefferson Davis Was a Conservative: The Missing Key to Understanding the
    American Civil War
Confederacy 101: Amazing Facts You Never Knew About America's Oldest Political Tradition
Confederate Blood and Treasure: An Interview With Lochlainn Seabrook
Everything You Were Taught About African-Americans and the Civil War is Wrong, Ask a Southerner!
Everything You Were Taught About the Civil War is Wrong, Ask a Southerner!
Give This Book to a Yankee! A Southern Guide to the Civil War For Northerners
Heroes of the Southern Confederacy: The Illustrated Book of Confederate Officials, Soldiers, and Civilians
Lincoln's War: The Real Cause, the Real Winner, the Real Loser
The Great Yankee Coverup: What the North Doesn't Want You to Know About Lincoln's War!
The Ultimate Civil War Quiz Book: How Much Do You Really Know About America's Most Misunderstood Conflict?
Women in Gray: A Tribute to the Ladies Who Supported the Southern Confederacy

CONFEDERATE MONUMENTS
Confederate Monuments: Why Every American Should Honor Confederate Soldiers and Their Memorials

CONFEDERATE FLAG
Confederate Flag Facts: What Every American Should Know About Dixie's Southern Cross
What the Confederate Flag Means to Me: Americans Speak Out in Defense of Southern Honor, Heritage, and
    History

SECESSION
All We Ask Is To Be Let Alone: The Southern Secession Fact Book

SLAVERY
Everything You Were Taught About American Slavery is Wrong, Ask a Southerner!
Slavery 101: Amazing Facts You Never Knew About America's "Peculiar Institution"

CHILDREN
Honest Jeff and Dishonest Abe: A Southern Children's Guide to the Civil War
Saddle, Sword, and Gun: A Biography of Nathan Bedford Forrest For Teens

NATHAN BEDFORD FORREST
A Rebel Born: A Defense of Nathan Bedford Forrest - Confederate General, American Legend (winner of the 2011
    Jefferson Davis Historical Gold Medal)
A Rebel Born: The Screenplay (film about N. B. Forrest)
Forrest! 99 Reasons to Love Nathan Bedford Forrest
Give 'Em Hell Boys! The Complete Military Correspondence of Nathan Bedford Forrest
I Rode With Forrest! Confederate Soldiers Who Served With the World's Greatest Cavalry Leader
Nathan Bedford Forrest and African-Americans: Yankee Myth, Confederate Fact
Nathan Bedford Forrest and the Battle of Fort Pillow: Yankee Myth, Confederate Fact
Nathan Bedford Forrest and the Ku Klux Klan: Yankee Myth, Confederate Fact
Nathan Bedford Forrest: Southern Hero, American Patriot - Honoring a Confederate Icon and the Old South
Saddle, Sword, and Gun: A Biography of Nathan Bedford Forrest For Teens
The God of War: Nathan Bedford Forrest As He Was Seen By His Contemporaries
The Quotable Nathan Bedford Forrest: Selections From the Writings and Speeches of the Confederacy's Most
    Brilliant Cavalryman

QUOTABLE SERIES
The Alexander H. Stephens Reader: Excerpts From the Works of a Confederate Founding Father
The Quotable Alexander H. Stephens: Selections From the Writings and Speeches of the Confederacy's First Vice
    President
The Quotable Jefferson Davis: Selections From the Writings and Speeches of the Confederacy's First President
The Quotable Nathan Bedford Forrest: Selections From the Writings and Speeches of the Confederacy's Most
    Brilliant Cavalryman
The Quotable Robert E. Lee: Selections From the Writings and Speeches of the South's Most Beloved Civil War
    General
The Quotable Stonewall Jackson: Selections From the Writings and Speeches of the South's Most Famous General
The Unquotable Abraham Lincoln: The President's Quotes They Don't Want You To Know!

CIVIL WAR BATTLES
Encyclopedia of the Battle of Franklin - A Comprehensive Guide to the Conflict that Changed the Civil War
Nathan Bedford Forrest and the Battle of Fort Pillow: Yankee Myth, Confederate Fact
The Battle of Franklin: Recollections of Confederate and Union Soldiers
The Battle of Nashville: Recollections of Confederate and Union Soldiers
The Battle of Spring Hill: Recollections of Confederate and Union Soldiers

CONSTITUTIONAL HISTORY
America's Three Constitutions: Complete Texts of the Articles of Confederation, Constitution of the United States of America, and Constitution of the Confederate States of America
The Articles of Confederation Explained: A Clause-by-Clause Study of America's First Constitution
The Constitution of the Confederate States of America Explained: A Clause-by-Clause Study of the South's Magna Carta

VICTORIAN CONFEDERATE LITERATURE
Rise Up and Call Them Blessed: Victorian Tributes to the Confederate Soldier, 1861-1901
Support Your Local Confederate: Wit and Humor in the Southern Confederacy
The God of War: Nathan Bedford Forrest As He Was Seen By His Contemporaries
The Old Rebel: Robert E. Lee As He Was Seen By His Contemporaries
Victorian Confederate Poetry: The Southern Cause in Verse, 1861-1901

ABRAHAM LINCOLN
Abraham Lincoln: The Southern View - Demythologizing America's Sixteenth President
Lincolnology: The Real Abraham Lincoln Revealed in His Own Words - A Study of Lincoln's Suppressed, Misinterpreted, and Forgotten Writings and Speeches
Lincoln's War: The Real Cause, the Real Winner, the Real Loser
The Great Impersonator! 99 Reasons to Dislike Abraham Lincoln
The Unholy Crusade: Lincoln's Legacy of Destruction in the American South
The Unquotable Abraham Lincoln: The President's Quotes They Don't Want You To Know!

NATURAL HISTORY
North America's Amazing Mammals: An Encyclopedia for the Whole Family
The Concise Book of Owls: A Guide to Nature's Most Mysterious Birds
The Concise Book of Tigers: A Guide to Nature's Most Remarkable Cats

PARANORMAL
Carnton Plantation Ghost Stories: True Tales of the Unexplained from Tennessee's Most Haunted Civil War House!
UFOs and Aliens: The Complete Guidebook

FAMILY HISTORIES
The Blakeneys: An Etymological, Ethnological, and Genealogical Study - Uncovering the Mysterious Origins of the Blakeney Family and Name
The Caudills: An Etymological, Ethnological, and Genealogical Study - Exploring the Name and National Origins of a European-American Family
The McGavocks of Carnton Plantation: A Southern History - Celebrating One of Dixie's Most Noble Confederate Families and Their Tennessee Home

MIND, BODY, SPIRIT
Autobiography of a Non-Yogi: A Scientist's Journey From Hinduism to Christianity (Dr. Amitava Dasgupta, with Lochlainn Seabrook)
Britannia Rules: Goddess-Worship in Ancient Anglo-Celtic Society - An Academic Look at the United Kingdom's Matricentric Spiritual Past
Christ Is All and In All: Rediscovering Your Divine Nature and the Kingdom Within
Christmas Before Christianity: How the Birthday of the "Sun" Became the Birthday of the "Son"
Jesus and the Gospel of Q: Christ's Pre-Christian Teachings As Recorded in the New Testament
Jesus and the Law of Attraction: The Bible-Based Guide to Creating Perfect Health, Wealth, and Happiness Following Christ's Simple Formula
Seabrook's Bible Dictionary of Traditional and Mystical Christian Doctrines
Sea Raven Press Blank Page Journal: For Reflections, Notes, and Sketches
The Bible and the Law of Attraction: 99 Teachings of Jesus, the Apostles, and the Prophets
The Book of Kelle: An Introduction to Goddess-Worship and the Great Celtic Mother-Goddess Kelle, Original Blessed Lady of Ireland
The Goddess Dictionary of Words and Phrases: Introducing a New Core Vocabulary for the Women's Spirituality Movement
Vintage Southern Cookbook: Delicious Dishes From Dixie

WOMEN
Aphrodite's Trade: The Hidden History of Prostitution Unveiled
Princess Diana: Modern Day Moon-Goddess - A Psychoanalytical and Mythological Look at Diana Spencer's Life, Marriage, and Death (with Dr. Jane Goldberg)
Women in Gray: A Tribute to the Ladies Who Supported the Southern Confederacy

REPRINTS
A Short History of the Confederate States of America (author Jefferson Davis; editor Lochlainn Seabrook)
Prison Life of Jefferson Davis (author John J. Craven; editor Lochlainn Seabrook)
Life of Beethoven (author Ludwig Nohl; editor Lochlainn Seabrook)
The New Revelation (author Arthur Conan Doyle; editor Lochlainn Seabrook)

Lochlainn Seabrook does not author books for fame and fortune, but for the love of writing and sharing his knowledge.

THE GODDESS DICTIONARY
OF WORDS & PHRASES

*Introducing a New Core Vocabulary
For the Women's Spirituality Movement*

LOCHLAINN SEABROOK
JEFFERSON DAVIS HISTORICAL GOLD MEDAL WINNER

Diligently Researched and Generously Illustrated
by the Author for the Elucidation of the Reader

1997

Sea Raven Press, Nashville, Tennessee, USA

THE GODDESS DICTIONARY OF WORDS & PHRASES

Published by
Sea Raven Press, Cassidy Ravensdale, President
Nashville, Tennessee, USA
SeaRavenPress.com • searavenpress@gmail.com

Copyright © text and illustrations Lochlainn Seabrook 1997, 2010, 2021 in accordance with U.S. and international copyright laws and regulations, as stated and protected under the Berne Union for the Protection of Literary and Artistic Property (Berne Convention), and the Universal Copyright Convention (the UCC). All rights reserved under the Pan-American and International Copyright Conventions.

PRINTING HISTORY
1st SRP paperback ed., 1st printing, June 1997; 2nd ed. 1st printing, July 2010;
3rd ed. 1st printing Nov. 2021 • ISBN: 978-0-9827700-3-0
1st SRP hardcover edition, 1st printing, Nov. 2021 • ISBN: 978-1-955351-11-9

ISBN: 978-0-9827700-3-0 (paperback)
Library of Congress Control Number: 2010930770

This work is the copyrighted intellectual property of Lochlainn Seabrook and has been registered with the Copyright Office at the Library of Congress in Washington, D.C., USA. No part of this work (including text, covers, drawings, photos, illustrations, maps, images, diagrams, etc.), in whole or in part, may be used, reproduced, stored in a retrieval system, or transmitted, in any form or by any means now known or hereafter invented, without written permission from the publisher. The sale, duplication, hire, lending, copying, digitalization, or reproduction of this material, in any manner or form whatsoever, is also prohibited, and is a violation of federal, civil, and digital copyright law, which provides severe civil and criminal penalties for any violations.

The Goddess Dictionary of Words and Phrases: Introducing a New Core Vocabulary for the Women's Spirituality Movement, by Lochlainn Seabrook. Includes an introduction, illustrations, index, endnotes, and bibliography.

ARTWORK
Front and back cover design and art, book design, layout, and interior art by Lochlainn Seabrook.
All images, image captions, graphic design, & graphic art copyright © Lochlainn Seabrook.
All images selected, placed, manipulated, cleaned, colored, tinted, and/or created by Lochlainn Seabrook.
Cover photo: Statue of the Greek Goddess Athena, Athens, Greece, by Yiannis Scheidt

All persons who approve of the authority and principles of Col. Lochlainn Seabrook's literary work, and realize its benefits as a means of reeducating the world concerning important facts left out of our history books, are hereby requested to avidly recommend his titles to others and to vigorously cooperate in extending their reach, scope, and influence around the globe.

This is a scholarly book on a spiritual topic. The author is neither promoting nor denigrating its subject matter.
PRINTED & MANUFACTURED IN OCCUPIED TENNESSEE, FORMER CONFEDERATE STATES OF AMERICA

Dea Optimo Maximo

DEDICATION

To You Know Who

EPIGRAPH

The Moon! Artemis! The great goddess of the splendid past of men! Are you going to tell me she is a dead lump?

D. H. Lawrence (1885-1930)

CONTENTS

Note to the Reader - 10

Introduction, by Lochlainn Seabrook - 11
  An Overview - 11
  Why This Book Is Important - 12
  The Inspiration Behind This Book - 14
  The Story Behind This Book - 17
  Our Androcentric Language - 25

ENTRIES

A - 37
B - 39
C - 43
F - 49
G - 51
H - 105
I - 109
L - 113
M - 117

O - 129
P - 131
Q - 133
R - 135
S - 137
T - 141
U - 143
V - 145
W - 147

Bibliography and Suggested Reading - 155
Index - 186
Meet the Author - 247
Col. Seabrook's Matriarchal Ancestry - 248
Learn More - 249

NOTE TO THE READER
Third Edition

ALWAYS DEEPLY INTERESTED in religion, spirituality, Christian mysticism, mythology, history, and language (among the latter, more specifically etymology, onomastics, anthroponymy, and toponymy), I originally wrote this book in 1997. It is now 2021, nearly a quarter of a century later. Not surprisingly, much has changed in the world since the 1990s. What was once considered a male-dominant American society (what I term "the Patriarchy" throughout this book) is fast disappearing, and in many ways is now nonexistent. Indeed, as an author, most of the businesses and companies I now deal with are either female-dominant or completely female owned and operated. Our culture is certainly much more female-oriented than it was 24 years ago; something akin, in my opinion, to a pre-matriarchy.

Ancient goddess figurines.

While the thrust of this work (increasing public awareness of our male-based language and encouraging the inclusion of new female terms) may not be as urgent in 2021 due to Western society's renewed interest in empowering women, *The Goddess Dictionary of Words and Phrases* remains topical. For the English language will always be masculine heavy and the facts about the prehistoric Matriarchate—as well as the ancient Patriarchal Takeover that weakened and eventually obliterated it—are still being ignored or even intentionally concealed by a majority of writers and educators. Thus my book continues to have a place in the world library of truth, knowledge, and wisdom. L.S., Autumn 2021.

INTRODUCTION

To the Second Edition
BY COLONEL LOCHLAINN SEABROOK

AN OVERVIEW

The Goddess Dictionary of Words and Phrases is chiefly an educational compendium of vital information regarding the universal deity known around the world for thousands of years as "Goddess." I will focus specifically on various androcentric or patriarchal terms, expressions, and maxims, from ancient to modern times. I have taken these and feminized (or emasculated) them, a process that has created a new core vocabulary of feministic Goddess-oriented words and phrases.

A number of my verbal inventions—many obviously playful and purely experimental—are what could rightfully be called "new old" words and phrases. That is, I am taking the God-based wording of our modern male-dominant vocabulary and simply returning it to its original prehistoric feminine form.

An example: I have taken the contemporary androcentric saying, "in the name of God," and changed it to, "in the name of Goddess." As we now know, the latter female form was already in use for thousands of years before the belief in a Father-God arose. After the Patriarchal Takeover (which began c. 4300 B.C.), however, misogynistic priests masculinized the phrase and suppressed the original feminine version. My book allows these ancient silenced expressions, dedicated to the *Magna Dea*, the Great Mother, to be brought back to life. And while some of the resulting words may be unwieldy, experimental, and even impractical, they benefit us in that they reveal the deeply masculine nature of Western religious terminology, as well as the dire need for linguistic inclusivity.

WHY THIS BOOK IS IMPORTANT

The Goddess Dictionary of Words and Phrases is extremely topical. With the rise of the Second Wave of Feminism, there has been an accompanying re-emergence of interest in female religion and all that is related to it, particularly the figure of the universal mother-deity called "Goddess."

This global interest in the feminine aspect of religion is embodied in two related movements: the Women's Spirituality Movement and the Goddess Reclamation Movement. Both cut across every social, economic, racial, political, and religious element of society. Even gender is not a factor: many men are just as interested in learning about Goddess culture and Goddess religion as women. I count myself among them—although I am not a feminist.

It is not surprising then that resuscitated forms of ancient feminine religion—such as Neo-Paganism—are again on the rise, or that today there are more people involved in Wicce (that is, Witchcraft, a modern remnant of the original Goddess religion) than at any other time in human history.

Everywhere one turns in our culture there are overt signs of an explosive new interest in feministic spirituality. Recently, for example, the CBC (Canadian Broadcast Corporation) aired a radio series entitled *The Return of the Goddess*, British Pagans have begun reclaiming and renaming ancient Goddess shrines, and New York City held what it called "The First Goddess Festival." Feminist scholars, activists, and artists are disseminating information about Goddess through a myriad of worldwide lectures, gallery exhibits, workshops, conferences, and celebratory events.

As early as 1897 Victorian Americans found fascination in Goddess, one result of which was the construction of an exact replica of the Goddess Athena's ancient Greek Temple, the Parthenon, in Nashville, Tennessee. The structure still stands as a monument to our innate attraction to the mother-figure. I live nearby and have visited it numerous times.

In these ways and many others, Goddess is returning to the consciousness of humanity, a deity once worshiped by every culture and society on Earth before her name was suppressed by the Patriarchate (the global male-dominant culture that first arose about 6,000 years ago).

Along with the re-emergence of the Women's Spirituality Movement, countless books have been written over the past twenty years about Goddess and her World. We have, for instance: *When God was a Woman*, *The Civilization of the Goddess*; *The Divine Feminine*, and *The White Goddess*, just to name a few.

Yet, with the reclamation of Goddess going on around the globe, and with the accompanying growth of Feminism, it has become increasingly clear that we lack a matricentric vocabulary through which these "new old" ideas might be expressed. In other words, the necessity of a feminine idiom, one that could replace the words and phrases of the Patriarchate, has become of paramount importance.

A number of academics and writers have moved in this direction, with various attempts to fill in the many gaping holes left in the English language by patriarchalists. For example, in her book *Gyn/Ecology: The Metaethics of Radical Feminism*, feminist Mary Daly includes an index of new words that she has coined. Along this same line, several feminist or gender-neutral reference books have been published by a myriad of writers. Among these are: *A Feminist Dictionary*; *The Elements of Nonsexist Usage*; and *A Woman's Thesaurus*.

There is something missing from these works, however: each deals almost exclusively with *secular* words.

What is needed now is a specific reference book for the newly burgeoning Women's Spirituality Movement, and its associated fields of Goddess archaeology, feminine psychology, and Goddess symbology; one that provides readers with feministic words of a *metaphysical* nature. *The Goddess Dictionary of Words and Phrases* is that reference tool.

THE INSPIRATION BEHIND THIS BOOK

As an author of books on, among other topics, feminine mythology and religion, I often find myself running up against the limitations of the phallogenic, patriarchally-driven language we call "English." Nowhere is this limitation more evident than in the areas of theology and mythology.

The three primary religions of the West—Judaism, Christianity, and Islam—are all, on the surface at least, wholly androcentric; and being patriarchally monotheistic, they worship a sole male deity known as "God the Father." With our male-dominant culture recognizing only a masculine father-figure as the Supreme Being, it is not surprising that nearly every area of the English language reflects an androcentric, often overtly misogynistic worldview.

In fact, we English speakers have only one word whose essence is female: the word blonde, and this is of French origin.

At the same time the English language contains thousands of words such as: manage, manager, management, mandate, mandatory, man-eater, maneuver, manipulate, manhandle, man-hour, man-day, man-year, manhunt, manpack, man-size, mantel, manikin, man-of-war, mandrake, manacle, manhole, man-made, manpower, mantrap, manual, manifest, manufacture, manuscript, man-to-man, and manslaughter; all which signify the depth of masculinization to which our language has been submitted. Indeed, none of the above words have any English corollaries for women.

For writers such as myself, whose subject matter often surrounds religion and myth, this is a serious deficiency. When I need a word or phrase that expresses the feminine aspect of divinity, I have only patriarchal phraseology to turn to. The word most commonly used for both female *and* male deities, for example, is the plural male noun, "gods."

More to the point, since the three Western monotheistic religions do not (openly) recognize Goddess in the first place, our entire vocabulary is God-based.

We will note here that only Catholicism has begrudgingly

admitted a powerful female figure, the Virgin Mary, into the all-male Christian Pantheon—but even here she is portrayed as little more than a mortal "god-bearer." Judaism and Islam long ago consigned their own Mother-Goddesses, Asherah and Allat respectively, to the religious scrapheap of old Pagan deities.

In fairness we should point out that the Mormons (the Church of Jesus Christ of Latter-Day Saints, or LDS), too recognize a female Supreme Being, one they refer to generically as "Mother in Heaven," or the "Heavenly Mother." However, this deity is not the same as the Virgin Mary. In fact, she is identical to the great universal Pagan Mother-Goddess, whose existence Mormons infer from a passage in the book of Genesis (1:27). Despite this recognition, Mormons do not acknowledge or discuss this belief in public, probably because, rightly, this would associate their church with Paganism instead of orthodox Christianity.

The Shakers, who also recognize the Divine Feminine, suffer from a similar affliction, leaving Westerners with a truly male-dominant language in the area of religion.

Our God-based vocabulary has given rise to such androcentric words as: "godly," "Heavenly Father," and the oxymoronic "god-mother." In turn, our one-sided lexicon has spawned such expressions as: "In God we trust," "The word of God," and "The kingdom of God."

For those who are involved in, interested in, or who merely want to write or talk about thealogy (as opposed to theology), or more specifically, the Women's Spirituality Movement, Goddess, Goddess culture, or female psychology, there are few, if any, legitimate words or phrases to describe the feminine experience or the feminine perspective.

In *The Goddess Dictionary of Words and Phrases* I have feminized the English language by introducing a core vocabulary of matrifocal words and aphorisms surrounding Goddess and female psycho-spirituality. With my book one will no longer need to struggle with male-slanted speech. A whole new gynocentric dialect will provide much-needed words like "goddessly," "Heavenly Mother," and the more correct "goddess-mother." In addition, we will now have such accurate phrases as: "In Goddess we trust," "The word of Goddess," and the "Queendom of Goddess," at our disposal.

THE STORY BEHIND THIS BOOK

An introduction to a reference book about Goddess must always begin with a single elementary question: who is Goddess? For in the modern West this powerful figure—the *only* Supreme Being worshiped by all of humanity between 500,000 and 4500 B.C.—has been largely either ignored, suppressed, or forgotten.

Even the study of Goddess (and female-based religions), a field known as thealogy, is almost completely disregarded by Westerners, even by theologians (experts in the study of God and male-based religions) and religious scholars, the latter being the very individuals who should be the most knowledgeable in this area.

Known under the various titles of the "Great Mother," the "Queen of Heaven," "Our Lady," and the "Universal Creatress," Goddess is a maternal figure that has headed every known religion, from the Middle Paleolithic Era to the Upper Neolithic, a span of some 500,000 years. This global female-prominent society is called the Matriarchate.

During the rule of the Matriarchate, as etymological, archaeological, mythological, and anthropological evidence shows, human society was matriarchal, matrifocal, matrilocal, gynocratic, matricentric, and matrilineal. The Matriarchate's social structure was communal, theacratic, endogamic, classless, egalitarian, and centered around temple life.

At the political heart of these early human societies was a supervising queen-priestess, or great clan mother, and a council of (normally twelve) women who acted as a governing body (making thirteen in all). The nucleus of all activity, whether social or religious, however, was a primordial female deity known simply as "Goddess" (every known culture and society has given her its own personalized local name).

Evidence of the Matriarchate and of a global Goddess Religion is extensive. Archaeologists have uncovered, for instance, small statuettes of Goddess numbering in the thousands. Incorrectly called "Venuses" by unenlightened (sex-oriented) anthropologists, these delicately carved objects reveal the true meaning of Goddess to the prehistoric mind: she was the sacred personification of vitalistic nature, of the Eternal Cosmos, of, in fact, life and all living things.

The Venus sculptures of the Cro-Magnon people and other subsequent cultures present a faceless woman with large pendulous breasts, a pregnant abdomen, shelf-like buttocks, wide flaring hips, thick trunk-like thighs, and a swollen triangular vulva. The message here is overt: with her magic procreative powers, Goddess is none other than the Mother of Life, whose maternal love may be invoked to bring beneficence, safety, fecundity, and prosperity to humanity. More specifically, as an all-generative divinity, she personifies the never-ending cycle of the renewal of life, seen in the trinitarian functions of birth, death, and rebirth.

The remains of Epipaleolithic and Neolithic peoples show a near obsession with Goddess veneration, manifesting in a multitude of archetypal symbols. Most prominent is the lunar crescent (☾), the very embodiment of Goddess and womankind, whose twenty-eight-day menstrual cycles perfectly match the twenty-eight-day lunations of the Moon.

The down-ward pointing triangle (▽), a symbol of the feminine pubic triangle (the source of life), was also a popular symbolic emblem representing Goddess. Prehistoric pottery, altars, plaques, pendants, figurines, temple models, thrones, theriomorphic sculptures, and farming instruments, as well as the walls of houses and caves, were richly decorated with such motifs, showing the profound extent to which Goddess was honored and artistically represented.

Revealingly, during this same time period, the phallus symbol is noticeable by its absence. Indeed, *not a single image of a male deity, or of even a rudimentary father-figure, appears in the art of any prehistoric people.* The reason for this is simple: every aspect of human existence was associated with the Great Mother. Thus, from 500,000 B.C. onward, we find only artistic representations of a great maternal figure.

This phenomenon is connected, in great part, to the fact that the biological knowledge of paternity was then wholly unknown. Women were thus considered parthenogenic, or self-fertilizing deities, who magically generated life within themselves. Here we find the prehistoric beginnings of the notion of the "virgin-mother," the Pagans' archetypal woman who gives birth without the aid of men.

The lack of prehistoric interest in either a paternal figure or a father-god was stimulated by other factors as well.

As has now been firmly established, the true nuclear family of all living primates consists merely of the mother and her offspring. The two-parent monogamous family unit is found *on occasion* in only a few primate species (for example, the gibbon), where this form of coupling has been genetically programmed.

The result is that none of the great apes, which includes humans, are naturally monogamous. In fact, fatherhood is not known among any of the higher primate species: primatologists have discovered that a male's chief—and only real—function is insemination of the female egg. Additionally, and only in rare instances, some primate males may engage in group protection from predators and communal food gathering.

Beyond these two elementary functions, the male plays little or no role in the primate social order. It is the mother-child matrix that forms not only the original nuclear family, but lies at the root of human civilization itself. (This also explains why most sexual relationships between women and men seldom endure for any length of time: the two genders of *Homo sapiens* are simply not biologically hardwired to form lifelong monogamous unions. To override this evolutionary programming we have had to introduce numerous often stringent social, cultural, and religious ideas and rules. Despite this, over 60 percent of all marriages in the West ultimately end in divorce.)

And so it was that in prehistoric cultures and societies, men were considered adjuncts to the family unit, not integral aspects of it. Little wonder then that there are no depictions of men in prehistoric art, such as kings, princes, chiefs, or gods. Instead, typical Paleolithic representations of men show them as hunters, guardians, sexual companions, and drone-like workers, all laboring under the auspices of Goddess and her thirteen-member all-female *collegia*.

From the current meager evidence the fossil record has given up to us, life in the Goddess World was relatively peaceful, for our early matriarchal ancestors were settled agriculturists living in agrarian village-communities. The governing societal *Zeitgeist* was egalitarian and operated under what has been termed a "gylany": an assembly of women and men headed by a council of women.

Befitting a polygamous pre-marriage culture, gender-exclusive cemeteries were the norm, with women buried on one side of the village, and men on the other. In addition, fossil evidence from this period reveals a complete absence of defensive structures (such as hill forts, palisades, and stone ramparts) and of weaponry used for killing other humans (such as daggers, spears, and halberds). Indeed, throughout the artwork of the Paleolithic and Neolithic, not a single depiction of warfare, or even murder, is to be found.

Under Goddess there was no division between the secular and the sectarian. All was sacred, religious, and sanctified. Even the script of the Goddess World was spiritual in nature. Invented by women some 8,000 years ago (2,000 years before the emergence of the Sumerian script, long inaccurately referred to as the "first" alphabet), the Goddess vocabulary system involved over 210 core signs, each intended to be read as a sacred hieroglyph.

It was, in essence, a form of communication enabling contact between Goddess and her human children. The Goddess script (as must have been the language based on it) was intensely feminine, replete with triangles, swirls, ovals, circles, meanders, crescents, V's, W's, Y's, M's, O's, dots, crosses, and swastikas (originally a symbol of Goddess' regenerative energy), all archetypal symbols of the Female Principle.

As archaeologist Marija Gimbutas and numerous other scientists have demonstrated, around the year 4300 B.C., the spiritual harmony of the gynocentric world of Goddess was shattered, however, by a momentous three-wave movement known as the "Patriarchal Takeover."

The first movement began with the migration of an aggressive horse-back-riding people out of southwestern Russia into Europe around 6,000 years ago. This culture, known as the Aryans, or Indo-Europeans, was war-like, patrilineal, and exogamic, with a clearly defined social hierarchy and a powerful warrior-class. Artwork from this period shows an abrupt change in symbolism, one detected from Greece all the way to Ireland, revealing the depth of penetration into Europe of the first wave of patriarchalists, or Kurgans, as they are more precisely called.

The patricentric Indo-Europeans eradicated the pubic triangle symbol and the lunar crescent of Goddess from society, and replaced them with the phallic symbol and the solar sign, emblems representing a new and powerful male deity: the Sky-God, or *Dyaus Pitar*: "Heavenly Father."

It was in this period, 4000 B.C. (about 6,000 years ago), that images of male gods flooded onto the artistic scene for the first time, while the sacred script of Goddess was replaced with an administrative script used solely for secular purposes. Defensive ditches and barricades, fortified villages, and hilltop fortresses now began appearing. In addition, burial evidence begins to show signs of human-on-human violence, and—along with the sudden appearance of daggers, maceheads, battle-axes, bows and arrows, and spearheads—we find mass graves filled with murdered women and children.

A strong trend away from a settled agrarian life to a highly mobile pastoral lifestyle emerged. The cooperative equalitarianism of the Goddess culture, with its *female-prominent* socialistic structure, disappeared, supplanted by a *male-dominant*, rigidly ranked hierarchy founded on physical strength and brute force. This new patriarchal society was governed, not by a communal-based gylanic council (as were the Goddess-worshipers, or Old Europeans), but by a single elite ruling family at whose head sat the

"Books invite all; they constrain none."
Hartley Burr Alexander (1873-1939)

male warrior-chieftain.

As wave after wave of Kurgan tribes thrust their way into the Goddess World, the practice of monogamy appeared for the first time. This was fueled by a new awareness of paternity, the result of experiments with animal breeding and the domestication of livestock by Kurgan men. Now, not only were gender-exclusive cemeteries replaced by male-dominated gender-inclusive cemeteries, but male burials became extremely rich in grave goods (for example, jewelry), while women were buried with little more than common everyday items (for example, leather shawls). Tellingly, women now began to be buried at the feet of male corpses instead of at their side.

It is clear that the status of the female had, by this time, been reversed, becoming inferior to that of the male, who now began to see her, not as a divine goddess in her own right—with magical procreative powers, but as a personal annoyance and a physical hindrance to his nomadic warrior lifestyle.

By 2500 B.C. the global Matriarchate and its Goddess Religion had collapsed, taken over by the Patriarchate, an androcentric, and often intensely violent, culture with diametrically opposed beliefs, customs, and ideologies to that of the Matriarchate.

By 500 B.C., in Greece, the ideas of skepticism, atheism, politics, and science had arisen, and with them, the belief in Goddess, spiritual rebirth, and the life-nurturing qualities of mythology, all but perished in the flames of the new Western scientific materialism.

OUR ANDROCENTRIC LANGUAGE

With human society now patricized, and with its energies directed from the Great Earth-Mother to the Great Sky-Father, it was only natural that human language would also pass through a profound masculinization process. And, in fact, this is precisely what occurred.

In Europe, for instance, the free-flowing feminine-looking script of Goddess was transformed into the more angular-shaped alphabet of the Minoan hieroglyphs, the Linear A script of Crete (called Eteocypriot), and finally into Classical Greek and Latin. The Indo-European speakers from Russia heavily impacted the feminine-sounding language of the Goddess World as well, as the new Europeans imposed themselves on the old Europeans.

To this day, conspicuous evidence of the linguistic imposition of the Patriarchy permeates every aspect of the English language, beginning with the word "English" itself: England and its dialect take their names from a fierce and bellicose male-dominant Germanic people known as the Angles, who, after conquering the British Isles in the 5th Century, gave the islands the name *Angle's Lænden*. Over the centuries this was corrupted from *Angleslænden*, to *Anglaend*, to "England." So significant was the Angle's impact on the language of Medieval England that to this day English is known to linguists as a "Germanic language."

Indeed, English as a whole is so overtly top-heavy with male-oriented words, that there can be little question of the existence of a pervasive and intensely misogynistic force at work during its creation and evolution. For example, we have: history ("his story"); testament, testify, and testimony (all related to the word "testicle"); seminar and seminal (related to the word "semen"); and person, personal, and personnel (which include the word "son," not "daughter").

Even everyday Anglo-Saxon surnames betray a male-oriented substructure: Johnson means "son of John," Matheson means "son of Matthew," and Anderson means "son of Andrew." Revealingly, in England at least, we have no feminine corollary surnames such as: Heatherdaughter—"daughter of Heather"; Amydaughter—"daughter of Amy"; or even Williamdaughter—"daughter of William."

This custom has carried over into Irish and Scottish culture as well, where one of the meanings of the cognate "Mc," or "Mac," is "son of." For example, the literal translation of MacDonald is "son of Donald." And in Wales boy's surnames were once prefixed with the Welsh word *Map* (later shortened to *Ap*) meaning "son," giving us such surnames as Apgwyn—"son of Gwyn," or Apphilip—"son of Philip."

What we are speaking of here is the Western custom of *patronymicism*, in which a child is named after the father instead of the mother. Before the Patriarchal Takeover, however, children were named after their mother, a practice called *matronymicism*. Revealingly, modern Scandinavian countries retain many matronymics from the ancient Matriarchate, such as Gandolfsdatter ("daughter of Gandolf"); Hrolfsdottir ("daughter of Ralph"); Eriksdottir ("daughter of Eric"); and Dagsdotter ("daughter of Dag").

There are other clues to the androcentric nature of our language. We have, for example, such words as: sports*man*ship, crafts*man*ship, horse*man*ship, snow*man*, first base*man*, police*man*, gingerbread *man*, fire*man*, milk*man*, fore*man*, fisher*man*, fresh*man*, lay*man*, door*man*, and the ubiquitous "*brother*hood of *man*kind." There are no corresponding words for women in the English language. Why, for example, do we never hear of the "sisterhood of womankind," of a "snowwoman," or of "sportswomanship"?

Our male-dominant language has even placed women and men under the same male heading: "man." This piece of patriarchal conceit has given rise to such oxymoronic phrases as "the family of Man." (One is led to wonder how men would feel if both genders of the human race were called "Woman".)

Even the words "wo*man*," "wo*men*," and "fe*male*," show a closer relationship with the human male than they do with the human female. In fact, our words for the human female insinuate that she is merely an aspect of the male, rather than a separate being in her own right. The development of this view was a necessary outgrowth of the male-invented Genesaic Creation Myth, in which a man, "Adam," curiously gives birth to a woman "Eve" (see Genesis 2:21-23), instead of the female giving birth to the male, as all mammals, including humans, do. As a result, some of the more radical feminists have begun spelling woman "womyn," and women "wimyn."

Remark must also be made of the fact that five of the seven days of our week are named after male deities: Sunday (Sun's Day), Tuesday (Tiw's Day), Wednesday (Woden's Day), Thursday

(Thor's Day), and Saturday (Saturn's Day). The two exceptions are Monday, or Moon's Day, named after Goddess in her lunar form, and Friday, or Frigg's Day, named after the Scandinavian Love-Goddess Frigg or Frigga.

The same holds true for seven of the nine planets in our solar system: Mercury, Mars, Saturn, Jupiter, Neptune, Uranus, Pluto, are all celestial personifications of male gods. The two exceptions here are the planet Venus, named after the Roman Sex-Goddess Venus, and the planet Earth, named after the Indo-European Mother-Earth-Goddess Erda.

Our species, which was given the (perhaps overly optimistic) title *Homo sapiens sapiens* ("wise wise man") by a man (the 18th-Century Swedish biologist Carolus Linnaeus), is known as a "hu*man*," a creature that belongs to the "*King*dom" (not the "*Queen*dom") of Animalia.

Not surprisingly, the sciences of conservation, farming and agriculture, and the control of domestic animals are collectively called "*husband*ry," while the overseer of these industries, whether it be a woman or a man, is called a *husbandman*. The modern definition of the word husband is "steward" or "administrator," a role that originally belonged to women, the actual inventors of agriculture and conservation.

The ancient meaning of husband, however, betrays the utter reversal that took place as the fallout from the Patriarchal Takeover suffused into every aspect of early human society, including language. Originally, husband referred to a man-servant (or more loosely, a farm manager) who was bound or bonded to a woman's house, the mistress for whom he worked: *hus* means "house," while *bund*, gives us the words "bond(ed)" or "bound." In other words, "house-bound."

There is more. We have, for instance, the "Church Fathers," our "Forefathers," the "Founding Fathers," and the "Sons of our Fathers." One never hears of the "Church Mothers," our "Foremothers," the "Founding Mothers," or the "Daughters of our Mothers" (though there were many of each).

We may also add to these words such phrases as: "man of God," "man of letters," "man of straw," "no man's land," "man of the house," and "man of the world." Our male-saturated, male-dominated, male-oriented language has led one social critic to call our culture "ego-testicle."

It is with English words related to religion, however, that we find the strongest evidence for a male-centered language.

The starting point here must be with the phrase, "the Man upstairs," a hint of the profound influence of the patriarchal Judeo-Christian-Islamic heritage on Western culture. (Interestingly, while Goddess was long ago entirely expurgated from these three faiths, each still retains traces of the Goddess Religion from out of which they were originally formed: Judaism still relies on Goddess' ancient thirteen-month Lunar Calender; Christianity converted the old Semitic Virgin-Mother-Goddess Mari into the "Virgin Mary"; and Islam's symbol still preserves Goddess' holy emblem, the lunar crescent.) One will never hear the phrase "the Woman Upstairs" in any contemporary church, temple, or synagogue.

Nothing, however, epitomizes our phallocentric language

more than the Bible (KJV) itself, as the following list aptly illustrates:

1. The word "man" appears 2,246 times in the Bible.
   The word "woman" appears only 339 times.
2. The word "men" appears 1,112 times in the Bible.
   The word "women" appears only 170 times.
3. The word "he" appears 7,608 times in the Bible.
   The word "she" appears only 728 times.
4. The word "him" appears 4,991 times in the Bible.
   The word "her" appears only 1,193 times.
5. The word "his" appears 5,791 times in the Bible.
   The word "hers" appears only 4 times.

Unfortunately, this global masculinization of religion has left a large, empty psychical space in the life of the human animal, a primate whose entire biopsychological complex is geared, not toward the male, but toward the maternal-figure; that is, the Great Mother. For as objective studies have repeatedly shown, all children innately see the mother as the primary parent; nearly all primate (and indeed nearly all mammalian) families are matriarchal in character; and the earliest religions (as we have seen) were naturally based on a maternal figure—one they regarded as parthenogenic; that is, as a virgin-mother. In essence, we are truly a matricentric species.

With the re-emergence of the Women's Spirituality Movement and the contemporary "invention" of feminine psychology, this psychic void is at last beginning to heal over as a new form of "Goddess Consciousness" begins to take hold of the human imagination once again. It is my hope that *The Goddess Dictionary of Words and Phrases* will aid in the development of these movements.

LOCHLAINN SEABROOK
Franklin, Tennessee, USA
Summer 2010

"The Mother of the Gods," by Del Mar.

Nymph relief from Gallipoli, Turkey.

Benten, the Japanese Goddess of Divine Love.

Venus, the Roman Goddess of Divine Love, with mirror.

THE GODDESS DICTIONARY

of

WORDS AND PHRASES

ENTRIES

The ancient Egyptian Virgin-Mother-Goddess Isis suckling the Divine Son-God or Sun-God, Horus. Many of Isis' traits and myths were later appended to the figure of the Virgin Mary.

Archaic Venus the Roman love-goddess in the Pompeian style.

Babylonian clay figurines of "the Lady," the great Mother-Goddess Beltis, consort of the great Father-God Bel.

A

AS WITH OUR MOTHERS, MAY GODDESS BE WITH US

(the patriarchal form is: "As with our fathers, may God be with us," the motto of Boston, Massachusetts)

In Massachusetts (and elsewhere) this, the matriarchal form, is used as a toast, blessing, farewell, or salutation, by Goddess-worshipers.

Ancient goddess statue.

The Semitic love-goddess Astarte, accompanied by three traditional female symbols: the triangle, twelve pine cones, and the lunar crescent "under her feet" (see Revelation 12:1-2).

B

BY JUNO! (the patriarchal form is: "By Jove!")

An expletive, this, the matriarchal form of the ancient androcentric version, is often invoked by modern Goddess-worshipers as an exclamatory phrase. Jupiter or Jove (in Latin, *Jovis Pater*, "Youthful Father"), was the pre-Christian Father-God of the Pagan Romans (in Greece he was known as Zeus), the same male Father-God who became "Jahe" or "Yahweh" in Judaism, and who later became "Jehovah," "Yeshua," or "Jesus," in Christianity. The phrase "by Juno!" derives from the fact that Juno is the consort-wife of Jove; that is, she is the feminine aspect of the Supreme Being.

As the Heavenly Mother of ancient Rome Juno was known variously as the "Blessed Virgin Mother," the "Queen of Heaven," and the "Mother of all humanity." Juno's sacred month is the month to which she gave her name: June. The custom of marrying in June is a relic left over from the ancient Pagan veneration of Juno who, for at least 2,500 years, has governed marriage and the family. Like all of the many great virgin-mothers, Juno gave birth to a savior-son-god. In this case it was the deity Mars.

Juno's name is related to the words uni (as in universe) and yoni, the Sanskrit word for vulva or vagina. In ancient times every Roman woman was said to have a "*juno*" within her, just as every man was believed to possess a "*genius*" (in Rome a "genius," that is, a spirit or jinn, a tutelary deity that watched over a person or place). A woman's inner juno then represents her feminine soul, the very essence of Goddess herself.

After the Patriarchal Takeover took hold in Rome, misogynistic men forced the word *juno* from the Latin vocabulary, in essence, denying women their souls. For centuries afterwards orthodox Christian Fathers held that "women are soulless," which is why even now women continue to be denied positions of authority in many Christian denominations.

To this day only the male-based word genius is used in everyday speech—for both men *and* women. Even the meaning of the word genius was changed by men to reflect what they believed to be their "mental superiority." Not surprisingly, Webster's (androcentric) dictionary merely defines Juno as "the wife of Jupiter." While the original meaning of the word *juno* continues to be suppressed by mainstream society, it is beginning to find usage once again among those involved in the Women's Spirituality Movement.

Indeed, the omnipotence of Juno has never been fully subdued. Many of Juno's attributes (for example, being parthenogenic), her sacred symbols, (for example, the three-lobed lily), and her titles (for example, the "Blessed Virgin Mother" and the "Queen of Heaven"), were later appended to the Christian version of Goddess, the Virgin Mary (respectively portrayed on the first edition of this book). Thus, Mary herself, like Juno and all other minor goddesses, is merely a local form of the Universal

Great Mother-Goddess, worshiped around the world for the past 500,000 years under a myriad of names. (See GODDESS; HEAVENLY MOTHER; QUEEN OF HEAVEN)

BY THE GRACE OF GODDESS (the patriarchal form is: "By the grace of God")

An ancient royal maxim applied to those women (and men) stepping up to the throne, as in "you are now made Queen, by the grace of Goddess." This, the matriarchal form, is used by Goddess-worshipers in place of the patriarchal version, to initiate new ventures.

Lakshmi, the Hindu female Supreme Being.

A Christian woodcut depicting the Virgin Mary in the traditional Pagan manner, as the "Queen of Heaven."

CHILD OF GODDESS (the patriarchal form is: "child of God")

This, the matriarchal form, is used by Goddess-worshipers in place of the patriarchal version to denote the reverential mother-child relationship that exists between Goddess and a human being. (See CHILDREN OF GODDESS; GODDESS' CHILD; GODDESS' CHILDREN; WOMAN OF GODDESS)

CHILDREN OF GODDESS (the patriarchal form is: "children of God," a phrase long used by patriarchalists, and commonly employed by biblical writers; see for example, Matthew 5:9; 1 John 5:2)

This, the matriarchal form, is used by Goddess-worshipers in place of the patriarchal version. In prepatriarchal times (that is, before the invention of the idea of the Father-God around 4300 B.C.), both women and men were thought of as the "children of Goddess." After the Patriarchal Takeover, however, the Earth-Mother was masculinized and recast as the Sky-Father.

Creation myths too were altered to reflect a belief in a male "Creator" rather than the original female Creatress. With the powers of procreation stolen from women and given to men, the phrase "children of Goddess" became "children of God." (See CHILD OF GODDESS; GODDESS' CHILD; GODDESS'

CHILDREN; WOMAN OF GODDESS)

CRONE, MOTHER, AND VIRGIN DAUGHTER (the patriarchal form is: "Father, Son, and Holy Ghost," a quote taken from the book of Matthew 28:19; see also 1 John 5:7)

This, the matriarchal form, is used by Goddess-worshipers in place of the patriarchal version.

The matriarchal form would seem to derive from the patriarchal one; that is, the all-male Christian Holy Trinity. But as with so many other aspects of Christianity, the opposite is true: the idea of the Trinity is a pre-Christian one that emerged from the matricentric Goddess-worshiping religions of the Paleolithic, Mesolithic, and Neolithic periods.

The number three is first and foremost to be associated, not with God and male religion, but with Goddess and female religion; for it correlates with Goddess' pubic triangle, or vulva (artistically represented like this: ▽), the downward-facing, three-pointed sacred orifice out of which all life is created. So primal is this symbol that it must certainly rank as humanity's earliest image of the Divine Feminine: crudely flaked stone triangles have been found in the fossil remains of hominids dating from as early as 500,000 B.C.

The image remains as vibrant today as it did in prehistoric times. It can still be seen, for example, as the downward-pointing triangle in the Jewish Seal of Solomon, or hexagramic Star of David. (It is commonly believed that the hexagram is an ancient emblem of Judaism. However, it was not adopted as such until the

17th Century, for its Pagan, feminine, and sexual imagery were well-known to ancient and Medieval orthodox Jewish authorities, who forbade its use as a "heathen symbol of human depravity.")

According to Hindu mythology, one day the "Yoni Yantra," the sacred triangle of the Goddess Devi (whose name was later demonized by Christian priests, becoming the "Devil"), gave birth to a spark of life: the fiery Male Principle, a Divine Son known as the "Lingam Yantra." This, the (erect phallic-like) upward-pointing masculine triangle (artistically represented like this: ∆), overlaid the downward-pointing feminine pubic triangle of the mother, forming a hexgramic union of sexual opposites (artistically represented like this: ✡) that mystics refer to as the Primal Androgyne, and which Hindus call Sri Yantra (the "Great Yantra").

In the Kabbalistic tradition Jewish mystics initiated a system of sex worship identical to Tantrism (the Hindu form of spiritual sex), which utilized the Great Yantra as its secret symbol. In this school of thought the hexagram came to be seen as a woman and a man in intimate embrace, signifying sexual-spiritual union with the Divine Feminine.

The number three has other female trinitarian associations, all which predate the rise of Christianity and the concomitant development of the masculine Holy Trinity.

From earliest times Goddess has been portrayed as possessing three chief roles: 1) the creator of life, 2) the preserver of life, and 3) the destroyer of life. From out of this view grew the image of her as a triadic entity, a Triple-Goddess in fact; one whose triplicate functions deal primarily with birth, life, and death (and/or resurrection).

In prehistoric and ancient art, the Triple-Goddess is often depicted as a composite deity whose triadic form manifests as:

1) a young virgin (the "Divine or Heavenly Child")
2) a middle-aged bride (the "Earth-Mother")
3) a widow, or grandmother (the "Underworld Crone")

The Triple-Goddess has had many names throughout human history, of course. Some of the more noted are:

▼ Parvati-Durga-Uma (India)
▼ Ana-Babd-Macha, or the Morrigan (Ireland)
▼ Hebe-Hera-Hecate (Greece)
▼ The Norns (the Vikings)
▼ The Fates (Roman)
▼ Diana Triformis (Druidic)
▼ Juventas-Juno-Minerva, or Uni (Latium)
▼ The Three Divine Sisters (pre-Columbian Mexico)
▼ The Three Marys (Gnostic Christian; see John 19:25, where a remnant of the Triple-Goddess Mary, or Mari, can still be seen)
▼ Luna-Diana-Proserpine or the Three Damosels (Medieval England)

After the Patriarchal Takeover (c. 4300 B.C.), the Triple-Goddess was partially, and then later, fully masculinized, giving rise to a host of mixed-gender, and finally, male-exclusive trinities. Among these are:

- Woden-Thor-Saxnot (Germanic)
- Osiris-Isis-Horus (Egyptian)
- Isis-Ra-El (Semitic; this trinity gave us the word Israel)
- Shamash-Sin-Ishtar (Babylonia)
- Helios-Selene-Aphrodite (Greece)
- Odin-Tyr-Frey (Scandinavian)

Finally, Christianity transformed the Crone-Goddess into God, the Mother-Goddess into Jesus, and the Virgin-Daughter into the Holy Ghost, creating the masculine Trinity: Father-Son-Holy Ghost, or Jehovah, Jesus, and the Holy Spirit. The Church even appropriated Goddess' sacred bird of peace, Columba, "the dove," which it thereafter used to represent the Holy Spirit (see for example, Matthew 3:16). (See GODDESSHEAD; GODDESS; THE SPIRIT OF GODDESS)

Sidonian coins with the Goddess of Navigation.

The Roman love-goddess Venus as victory.

F

FEAR OF GODDESS, THE (the patriarchal form is: "the fear of God")

    A phrase indicating the power of the Supreme Being. This, the matriarchal form, is used by Goddess-worshipers in place of the patriarchal version.

FOR GODDESS' SAKE (the patriarchal form is: "for God's sake")

    An exclamatory phrase invoking the name, beneficence, and purpose, of the Supreme Being. This, the matriarchal form, is used by Goddess-worshipers in place of the patriarchal version.

FOR THE GREATER GLORY OF GODDESS (the patriarchal form is: "For the greater glory of God," the motto of the Society of Jesuits)

    This, the matriarchal form, is used by Goddess-worshipers in place of the patriarchal version, as a toast at feasts and at social gatherings and religious services.

FROM GODDESS AND THE QUEEN (the patriarchal form is: "From God and the King," an ancient patriarchal method of signing royal documents)

    This, the matriarchal form, is used by Goddess-worshipers

in place of the patriarchal version, as a signature on both official documents and in personal correspondence.

A kylix showing Venus on the swan.

GLORY BE TO GODDESS ON HIGH (the patriarchal form is: "Glory be to God on high" a paraphrased quote taken from the orthodox Judeo-Christian holy book, Luke: 2:14; 19:38)

This, the matriarchal form, is used by Goddess-worshipers in place of the patriarchal version, as a salutation or toast.

GLORY OF GODDESS, THE (the patriarchal form is: "the glory of God," a phrase taken from the orthodox Judeo-Christian holy book, the Bible; see for example, Acts 7:55)

This, the matriarchal form, is used by Goddess-worshipers in place of the patriarchal version, as a tribute honoring the feminine aspect of the Supreme Being.

GLORY OF THE LADY, THE (the patriarchal form is: "the glory of the Lord," a phrase taken from the Judeo-Christian holy book, the Bible; see for example, 1 Kings 8:11)

This, the matriarchal form, is used by Goddess-worshipers in place of the patriarchal version, as a recognition of the handiwork of Goddess.

GLORY TO GODDESS ALONE (the patriarchal form is: "Glory to God alone")

This, the matriarchal form, is used by Goddess-worshipers in place of the patriarchal version, as a toast, or as a part of religious ceremonies.

GODDESS (the patriarchal form is: "God")

A noun which is literally defined as "the Ultimate Reality," but more often refers to a minor female deity, or more commonly as the Supreme Being in feminine form. From a psychological perspective the concept of Goddess is seen as the female aspect of one's Real Self or Higher Self. This, the matriarchal form, is used by Goddess-worshipers in place of the patriarchal version.

Since humans are born of the union of female and male, it is obvious that the psyches of both women and men are bisexual; that is, they contain a feminine energy system and a masculine energy system. These two systems appear to us as archetypes, which in mythology, dreams, and fairy tales, are most often personified in the figures of a Mother-Goddess and a Father-God, respectively.

It is well-known among depth psychologists that "Goddess" (or any female deity) symbolizes the feminine half of a woman's psyche and the feminine half of a man's psyche (the *anima*), while "God" represents the masculine half of a woman's psyche and the masculine half of a man's psyche (the *animus*).

It is herein that we see what could be considered a psychological instability inherent in the three great patriarchal monotheistic religions—Judaism, Christianity, and Islam—whose beliefs center on a single male deity, known respectively as

"Yahweh," "Jehovah," and "Allah": without a female deity or maternal figure-head, men have no archetype through which to express their feminine side, while women have only a male figure through which to express their masculine side. In other words, monotheistic religions (being patriarchal) completely disregard 50 percent of what makes up the total psyche of both women and men.

This imbalance of energy, heavily weighted toward the masculine end of the spectrum, forms the basis of many types of neurosis for women and men alike. More specifically, the splintering of the Real Self is the cause of the abuse or neglect of one's unconscious female and male archetypes. Polytheistic religions, of course, create no such problems, for—in their recognition and veneration of a multitude of both Goddesses and Gods—they nurture and express both the psyche's feminine energy system and its masculine energy system.

Interestingly, before the beginning of the Patriarchal Takeover (c. 4300 B.C.), the idea of a solitary male deity was non-existent; in other words, there was no such concept of "God." No images of male deities, or even father-figures, appear in any prehistoric art.

In stark contrast to this phenomenon, untold thousands of artistic images and symbols of a great maternal-figure appear around the globe from about 500,000 B.C. onward, a period best described as "the Goddess World," or more scientifically as "the Matriarchate." One of the many manifestations of the Goddess world was, of course, a spiritual belief system centered on the female, or more specifically, on the mother (matricentric religion), who early peoples personified as "Goddess." In the earliest stages of the Goddess Religion she was depicted in the carved shape of a simple three-sided stone, a symbol of her life-giving pubic-triangle.

Beginning about 35,000 B.C., artistic representations of Goddess began to portray her as an anthropomorphic mother-deity, with a featureless face (to symbolize her universality), large pendulous breasts, thick trunk-like thighs, a pregnant abdomen, an overtly swollen vulva, and large shelf-like buttocks. (As mentioned, supposing them to be of a sexual, even pornographic, nature—manufactured for the sensual pleasure of men—these images have long been incorrectly called "Venuses" by patriarchal anthropologists. In truth, these prehistoric images of Goddess, which straightforwardly proclaim her primordial function as the Great Creatrix of Life, are of a profoundly spiritual nature, and were no doubt used in religious rituals.)

It is plain to see then that for at least the past 500,000 years of human development—up until 6,000 years ago—all humans worshiped a sole maternal-figure who, long before the rise of Judaism, Christianity, or even of ancient Egypt, was known across the ancient world as the "Supreme Virgin-Mother and Creatress of the Universe and All Living Things."

Despite the fact that nearly all contemporary orthodox Christians refute the idea of a female Supreme Being (the Mormons are a rare exception to this rule), 2,000 years ago, the first Christians—the Gnostics, were ardent devotees of Goddess, whom they called "The One." And if we are to believe the claims of modern alien abductees (known to ufologists as "experiencers"), extraterrestrial beings (whom abductees often liken to the angels of biblical mythology) operate under the sole tutelage of an all-powerful female figure, whom they also call "The One." If true, the ramifications of this connection between the earliest Christians and modern alien abduction reports are quite astounding to contemplate.

With such a long unbroken tradition of Goddess-worship, dating from the Paleolithic into the present, we should not be surprised to learn that the very word "God" derives from a prepatriarchal Hindu female deity named Goda, known in Scandinavian mythology as the Light-Goddess Gerd, in Gothic mythology as the River-Goddess Godavari, and in British mythology as the fertility-Goddess Lady Godiva.

After the Patriarchal Takeover male deities began to emerge in the various religious myths of the world for the first time. It was during this period that Goddesses obtained male consorts, male servants, and male guardians, each of whom men called "God," again, a masculinization of the name of the Great Mother-Goddess, Goda. In Hindu mythology, Goda's male consort was named Godan, in Norse legend he was called Odin, in Gothic myth he was named Father Goth, and in Saxon and Frankish mythology he was called Woden or Wotan, after whom our weekday Woden's Day, or rather "Wednesday," is named.

Goddess had, and continues to have, many personifications, functions, and figures. These are epitomized in the literally millions of names she has been given by various cultures, religions, societies, cults, and civilizations, throughout human prehistory right into the present day. Indeed, every nation on Earth has venerated, or continues to venerate, one or more goddesses, each a local personification of the Great Goddess herself.

A highly abbreviated list of some of the world's major Goddesses would include:

▼ Acca Larentia (Etruria)
▼ Achtan (Ireland)
▼ Adath (Canaan)
▼ Aida-Wedi (Haiti)
▼ Aisha Qandisha (Morocco)
▼ Akewa (Argentina)
▼ Akka (Turkey)
▼ Ale (Nigeria)
▼ Allat (Arabia)
▼ Aphrodite (Greece)
▼ Asherah (Semitic: Judaism)
▼ Bridget (Celtic)
▼ Coatlicue (Mexico)
▼ Diana (Italy)
▼ Eriu (Ireland)
▼ Eve (Semitic: Judeo-Christian)
▼ Haltia (Balkan)
▼ Imd (Scandinavia)
▼ Isis (Egypt)
▼ Ixtab (Central America: Maya)

▼ Kali (India)
▼ Kelle (Celtic; as I reveal in my work *The Book of Kelle*, she gave her name to the Kelts or Celtic people)
▼ Kupalo (Russia)
▼ Lilwani (Babylonia: Hittite)
▼ Lorop (Micronesia)
▼ Louhi (Finland)
▼ Mari (Semitic)
▼ Mary (Semitic: Judeo-Christian)
▼ Matergabiae (Lithuania)
▼ Mawu (Africa)
▼ Nicnevin (Scotland)
▼ Ninsar (Sumeria)
▼ Ognyene Maria (Serbia)
▼ Orore (Chaldea)
▼ Oshun (Brazil)
▼ Paive (Norway)
▼ Pao-Yueh (China)
▼ Qocha Mana (North America: Hopi)
▼ Rachel (Semitic: Judeo-Christian)
▼ Ri (Phoenicia)
▼ Saris (Armenia)
▼ Satine (Indonesia)
▼ Scotia (Scotland)
▼ Sibilaneuman (Columbia)
▼ Sinjang Halmoni (Korea)
▼ Sophia (Gnostic Christian)

- ▼ Srinmo (Tibet)
- ▼ Teleglen Edzen (Mongolia)
- ▼ Unelanuhi (North America: Cherokee)
- ▼ Uti Hiata (North America: Pawnee)
- ▼ Utset (North America: Navaho)
- ▼ Viviane (Wales)
- ▼ Wah-Kah-Nee (North America: Chinook)
- ▼ Wakahirume (Japan)
- ▼ Waramurungundji (Australia)
- ▼ Wilden Wip (Germany)
- ▼ Xatel-Ekwa (Hungary)
- ▼ Xochiquetzal (Central America: Aztec)
- ▼ Yak (Malaysia)
- ▼ Yemaya (Hispanic: Santeria)
- ▼ Zima (Slavonia)
- ▼ Zywi (Poland)

Goddess' most popular name, however, derives from her association with the sea and her function as the Great Mother whose oceanic love poured out onto the world during the initial divine act of creation. (Science has verified this notion: the fossil record shows that all life on Earth originally arose from the sea some 3.8 billion years ago).

A woman's salty amniotic fluid, her foamy white breast milk, and her briny menstrual blood (nearly chemically identical to seawater)—and the connection these things have with the life-bearing powers of the female—also link Goddess (and all women) to the ocean. This is why the Indo-European root for sea is *mar*, which is a play on the Indo-European root-word *ma*, meaning "mother." In Latin, for instance, *mare* or *maris*, both refer to the sea and seawater; *marina* means "of the sea"; and *maritimus* (maritime) means "seafaring." In Latin the Mediterranean Sea is called *Mare Nostrum* ("Our Mother-Ocean"), while the half-woman, half-fish marine creature of popular lore is still known as a mermaid (from the Old English word *mere*, "sea"). Hence, we find a host of Goddess names beginning with the cognate "mar" or "mer" dating as far back as the Neolithic.

For example, to the early Syrians, Goddess was called Meri; to the ancient Jews she was Marah (or Miriam); and to the Chaldeans she was Marratu. The Persians knew Goddess as Mariham; the Amorites as Mari; the Saxons as Wudu-Maer; and to the Scandinavians she was Maerin.

One of the names given to Goddess by the ancient Egyptians was Mer; to the Slavs she was Marzanna; to East Indians she is Kali Ma; in Latium she was Marica; and in ancient Rome she was sometimes known as Maria. Asians have known her as either Mara or Maya, while to the ancient Greeks she was called Maia.

To the Medieval Celto-Britons Goddess was Maid Marian; the African Fon call her Mawu; ancient Iran knew her as Mariana; the Akkadians referred to their Mother-Goddess as Lady Marri. To later-emerging Gnostic and orthodox Christians, she was, of course, known as Mary.

Whatever her name, figure, legend, or function, the consensus among her devotees is that Goddess is alive and well, and that she is slowly returning to reclaim her lost followers, reestablish her Church, and set about healing the open psycho-spiritual wound left by patriarchalists and their male-oriented, God-centered religions.

As such, it is not surprising that the word "God" is everywhere beginning to once again be replaced by, or used in conjunction with, the word "Goddess," the very subject of this dictionary. (See GODDESS CREATED THE HEAVEN AND THE EARTH; GODDESS THE CREATRESS; HEAVENLY MOTHER; MOTHER)

GODDESS' ACRE (the patriarchal form is: "God's acre")

This, the matriarchal form, is used by Goddess-worshipers in place of the patriarchal version, to refer to the area surrounding a Goddess temple, shrine, or sanctuary. It may also be used to indicate a churchyard.

GODDESS ALMIGHTY (the patriarchal form is: "God almighty," a phrase long used by the Patriarchy, and commonly employed by biblical writers; see for example, Exodus 6:3)

This, the matriarchal form, is used in place of the patriarchal version. Like many phrases and words now routinely associated with the Father-God of the Patriarchate, etymology reveals that the origins of the word-title "Almighty" derive directly from the Goddess Religion of the old Matriarchate. Evidence for this is found in the Bible itself.

In every one of the forty-eight occurrences of the English

word "almighty" in the Old Testament, the original Hebrew word is *shaddai*, or rather *El Shaddai*, a word-title meaning "a milk-giving breast," "the nursing mother," or more precisely, the "Great Mountain-Mother-Goddess" (see for example, Genesis 17:1; Psalms 91:1).

The symbolism here is clear: the mountain, especially the snow-capped mountain, has long been viewed as a psychic archetype of the milk-spouting, life-nurturing female breast, itself a symbol of the Great Goddess in her reproductive role as a maternal life-bearing mother.

"Magic mountains" are common motifs in myth and fairy tales, where witches (demonized priestesses of the Goddess Religion) play, and where the mountains themselves "give birth" to great deities, or serve as the home of goddesses and gods. Hence, in ancient times *El Shaddai* was the generic name-title for any type of Semitic mountain-goddess.

Later, when Medieval English scribes, working under the auspices of my Scottish cousin King James (1566-1625), set about to translate the Bible into English, they intentionally mistranslated the Hebrew word *Shaddai* as "Almighty" (meaning "omnipotent") in an effort to obscure its Pagan feminine origins.

We know, however, that like so many other ancient cultures, prepatriarchal Jews not only venerated mountains as personifications of the Great Life-Giving Mother (whom they called Asherah), but also as her milk-giving breasts, her distended pregnant abdomen, and her swollen *mons veneris* ("Mound of Venus")—the life-giving vulva.

It is little wonder then that the ancient Jews often lingered on and around what they called *Har Elohim*, or "the Mount of God," a place-name which, literally translated from the original Hebrew, means: "the Mount of Goddess"; that is, "the pregnant belly of the Mountain-Mother" (see for example, Exodus 4:27; 1 Kings 19:8). (See MOUNT OF GOD)

GODDESS' ANGER (the patriarchal form: "God's anger," a phrase long used by the Patriarchy, and commonly employed by biblical writers; see for example, Numbers 22:22)

This, the matriarchal form, is used by Goddess-worshipers in place of the patriarchal version, to refer to Goddess' wrathful side.

GODDESS-AWFUL (the patriarchal form is: "god-awful")

An adjective used by Goddess-worshipers to describe the quality or state of something or someone that is extremely disagreeable. This, the matriarchal form, is used in place of the patriarchal version.

GODDESS BE PRAISED (the patriarchal form is: "God be praised")

This, the matriarchal form, is used by Goddess-worshipers in place of the patriarchal version, as a salutation in honor of the Supreme Being, Goddess.

GODDESS BE WITH YE (YOU) (the patriarchal form is: "God be with ye")

An ancient farewell used as a concluding remark or gesture toward parting company. Our modern English word, the noun good-bye, is a corrupted derivation of this 16th-Century English phrase, which ultimately derived from the ancient feminine phrase: "Goddess be with ye."

This, the matriarchal form, is used by contemporary Goddess-worshipers in many ways in place of the patriarchal version, from personal correspondence to religious rituals. (See GOODDESSBYE)

GODDESS BLESS AMERICA (the patriarchal form is: "God bless America")

This, the matriarchal form, is used by Goddess-worshiping citizens of the United States of America in place of the patriarchal version, as a prayer of solicitation asking for Goddess' protection.

GODDESS BLESS YOU (the patriarchal form is: "God bless you")

This, the matriarchal form, is used by Goddess-worshipers in place of the patriarchal Christian version, which Christianity long ago adopted from the ancient Pagan masculine expression, "Jupiter preserve you."

The phrase itself originally derives from the prepatriarchal belief that Goddess gave birth to all life with her breath, or through her spoken word, called by pre-Christian Greek Pagans, the *Hieros Logos*, or the "Holy Word." This led to the idea that one's soul is made of air and, in turn, to the notion that the soul may fly out of one's open mouth during a yawn, cough, or sneeze.

Evidence of this fact can be seen in the Indo-European word *atman,* which means "soul," or more correctly, "breath-soul." This cognate is found throughout the Indo-European family of languages: the German word for "breath" or "air," for instance, is *atmen*, while our word "atmosphere" derives from the Greek word for "air," *atmos*. According to the ancient Polynesian Creation Myth, the Supreme Being molded humans from dirt and animated them with a soul by breathing on them. Hence, the Polynesians call their "first man" *Tiki-Ahua*, meaning "The Creator's Sneeze."

The early patriarchal Jews borrowed on these ideas and expertly wove them into their own Creation Myth. To this day we may still read in the canonical Bible of how the Judeo-Christian Father-God, Yahweh, created humanity solely by breathing on a molded clump of dirt (see Genesis 2:7). The name of the first man created thus? *Adamah* or "Adam," the Jewish version of the far older Pagan *Atman* or *Ahua*.

These ancient Pagan beliefs live on in other ways as well.

Covering the mouth while yawning or coughing, for instance, is a vestigial custom left over from the time when Goddess-worshiping people thought that they must cover the mouth to prevent the soul from leaping out. Likewise, the custom of saying "Goddess/God bless you" after a sneeze is little more than a truncated prayer which offers last rites in case the soul manages to make good its escape.

While most Christians seem oblivious to the Pagan origins

of this now Christianized expression, Jews have long known otherwise, which is why the Talmud bans the custom of saying "Goddess/God bless you" as a gross superstition. (See WORD OF GODDESS, THE; GODDESS CREATED THE HEAVEN AND THE EARTH; SPIRIT OF GODDESS, THE)

GODDESSCHILD (the patriarchal form is: "godchild")

A noun referring to a person for whom another person becomes a sponsor at baptism. Goddess-worshipers use this, the matriarchal form, in place of the patriarchal version.

GODDESS' CHILD (the patriarchal form is: "God's child")

This, the matriarchal form, is used by Goddess-worshipers in place of the patriarchal version, to refer to one who views Goddess as their Divine Mother. (See CHILD OF GODDESS; CHILDREN OF GODDESS; GODDESS' CHILDREN)

GODDESS' CHILDREN (the patriarchal form is: "God's children")

This, the matriarchal form, is used by Goddess-worshipers in place of the patriarchal version, to refer to those who believe Goddess to be their Divine Mother. (See CHILD OF GODDESS; CHILDREN OF GODDESS; GODDESS' CHILD)

GODDESS CREATED THE HEAVEN AND THE EARTH (the patriarchal form is: "God created the heaven and the earth," a phrase taken from the Judeo-Christian holy book, the Bible; see

Genesis 1:1)

 This, the matriarchal form, is used in place of the patriarchal version. The Patriarchy has long contended that their male Father-God—whether he be called Zeus, Jupiter, Baal, Ra, Brahman, Yahweh, or Jehovah—was the "Creator of the Universe."

 Actually, the earliest creation myths speak instead of a female "Creatress" called the "Great Virgin Mother-Goddess," who gave birth to the Cosmos and all living things. This certainly makes far more sense, since it is the female, not the male, who gestates and gives birth to new life, and who—along with her child—actually forms the nuclear family in nearly every mammalian species.

 Only among wolves do we find the practice and existence of fatherhood and the idea of paternity, and even here, it is genetically programmed. In every other mammalian species, fatherhood is either entirely absent, or it is a learned behavior.

 Objective anthropologists, primatologists, and sociologists know, for example, that in humans fatherhood is not instinctual. It is, as Margaret Mead once referred to it, a recent cultural invention. This is why a man must be intensely and repeatedly socialized to be a boyfriend, husband, and father. Women need no such socialization for motherhood: they are born with a powerful maternal instinct (feminists please note: Mother-Nature was the original "sexist," for it was she, not men, who gave the womb to females) which is activated by maternal role models during youth. (Hence, studies reveal that girls raised by non-maternal mothers typically do not make good mothers, despite the fact that they are genetically preprogrammed with a maternal instinct.)

With the woman being the natural head of the family, it is not surprising to learn that for thousands of years prior to the writing of the Bible, long before even the emergence of Judaism or Christianity, the feminine Creation myth of Goddess the Creatrix was the only one known from Oceania, Asia, and Africa, to the Americas, Europe, and the Middle East.

Among these cultures the pre-biblical legend of Goddess' great creation took many forms, of course. But the same feminine-maternal theme runs throughout each one.

In Greek Olympian cosmology, for example, it was Goddess—in the form of "Mother Earth"—not God, who brought life into being. As the ancient Grecian mythographers wrote:

> At the beginning of all things Mother Earth emerged from Chaos and bore her [divine] son Uranus as she slept. Gazing down fondly at her from the mountains, he showered fertile rain upon her secret clefts, and she bore grass, flowers, and trees, with beasts and birds proper to each. This same rain made the rivers flow and filled the hollow places with water, so that lakes and seas came into being.

The early Pelasgians had a similar pre-biblical creation story, one in which Goddess—here named Eurynome—bears the "Light of Life":

> In the beginning, Eurynome, the Goddess of All Things, rose naked from Chaos, but found nothing substantial for her feet

to rest upon, and therefore divided the sea from the sky, dancing lonely upon its waves. She danced towards the south, and the wind set in motion behind her seemed something new and apart with which to begin a work of creation.

Wheeling about, she caught hold of this north wind, rubbed it between her hands, and behold! the great serpent Ophion. Eurynome danced to warm herself, wildly and more wildly, until Ophion, grown lustful, coiled about those divine limbs and was moved to couple with her. . . . So Eurynome was . . . got with child.

Next, she assumed the form of a dove, brooding on the waves and, in due process of time, laid the Universal Egg. At her bidding, Ophion coiled seven times about this egg, until it hatched and split in two. Out tumbled all things that exist, her children: sun, moon, planets, stars, the earth with its mountains and rivers, its trees, herbs, and living creatures.

(Students of the Bible will notice a number of elements in this story that were later borrowed by ancient Hebrew mythographers and appended to the legend of Adam and Eve.)

Other Grecian creation myths show Goddess, not God, giving birth to the world. Homer, for instance, said that "all living creatures originated in the stream of [the God] Oceanus which girdles the world, and that [the Goddess] Tethys was the mother of all his children." The mystical Orphics held that

> black-winged Night, a goddess of whom even Zeus stands in awe, was courted by the wind and laid a silver egg in the

womb of darkness; and that Eros, whom some call Phanes [that is, the Sun or "the Son"], was hatched from this egg and set the Universe in motion.

To the ancient Mesopotamians it was Aruru, the "Bright Mother of the Hollow," who was the Creatrix who "formed everything." In ancient Egypt, it was Goddess, not God, who

> was the Being eternal and infinite, the creative and ruling power of heaven, earth, and the underworld, and of every creature and thing in them. . . . Mother-goddess, lady of heaven, queen of the gods . . . who raised up Tem in primeval time, who existed when nothing else had being, and who created that which exists . . . the greatest power on earth, who commandest all that is in the universe, and who preservest all the gods . . . the God-mother, giver of life. . . . All that has been, that is, and that will be.

Before it was masculinized then, the original Judeo-Christian Creation myth no doubt read something like this:

> In the beginning, Goddess created the heaven and the earth. And the earth was without form, and void; and darkness was upon the face of the deep. And the Spirit of Goddess brooded upon the face of the waters.
> And Goddess said, "Let there be light." And there was light. And Goddess saw the light, that it was good: and Goddess divided the light from the darkness. And Goddess called the light "Day," and the darkness She called "Night."
> And Goddess said, "Let there be a firmament in the

midst of the waters." And Goddess called the firmament "Heaven." And Goddess said, "Let the waters under the heaven be gathered unto one place, and let the dry land appear." And it was so.

And Goddess called the dry land "Earth," and the gathering of the waters She called "Seas." And Goddess saw that it was good.

Then Goddess said, "Let the Earth bring forth grass, and let there be lights in the firmament to divide the day from the night; and let them be for signs [astrology], and for seasons, and for days, and years." And Goddess made two great lights; the greater to rule the day; and the lesser to rule the night. She made the stars also. And Goddess saw that it was good.

Then Goddess said, "Let the Earth bring forth living creatures." And it was so. And Goddess saw that it was good.

Finally She said, "Let me make human beings in My image, after My likeness." So She created human beings in Her own image, in the image of Goddess created She them; female and male created She them. And Goddess blessed them, and looking around, She saw everything She had made, and behold, it was very good.

To some modern readers, these well-known passages from the book of Genesis may seem strange and ungainly when the word "God" is replaced throughout with the word "Goddess." Yet, this is precisely how the original Near Eastern Creation Myth was worded before patriarchal Jewish priests, living between 900 and 500 B.C., rewrote it from a male point of view—to fit their androcentric outlook.

The Bible itself still contains clues to the feminine character of the original Judeo-Christian Creation myth.

In the book of Isaiah, for example, we read that God created humanity from "the womb" of the Great Goddess (Isaiah 44:2), while the book of Genesis speaks of God forming "man of the dust of the ground." The "ground" here is, of course, Mother Earth; that is, Goddess (Genesis 2:7).

Most revealing is Chapter One, verse two of Genesis. The King James version reads: "And the Spirit of God moved upon the face of the deep." But this is a terrible translation (by King James' copyists) of an intentional mistranslation made by emerging ancient patriarchal Hebrew scribes in the 1st Millennium B.C. For, wishing to eradicate all traces of matriarchal Judaism from the Torah, they took the original prepatriachal Hebrew Goddess Creation myth and masculinized it. This biblical passage itself retains the evidence of this subterfuge.

To begin with, ancient peoples—being Goddess-worshipers—imaged the Spirit (or the Soul) as feminine, not masculine. This is why nearly all of the ancient words for "spirit" are feminine. We have, for example, the Greek words *pneuma* and *psyche*, and the Latin words *anima* and *alma*. All four are feminine words meaning "spirit" or "soul."

In Old English the words for mother (*modor*), maternal or motherly (*modorlic*), and womb (*modorhrif*) all begin with the Old English word for "spirit": *mod*. And in Hebrew the feminine word for "the Spirit" is *ruwach*, which can also mean "wind," "breath," or "life." In many early Creation myths, Goddess creates life by blowing on, or speaking to, inanimate objects (here we have the origin of the concept of "the Word made flesh," or the *Logos*; that is, "the Word"). The "Spirit" mentioned in Genesis 1:2 then is a creative feminine deity; that is, Goddess.

As for the Genesaic word "moved," the original Hebrew here is *rachaph*, which means to "brood," clearly a *female* activity: the Old English word *brod* or brood, means "to sit on and incubate, or hatch, eggs." The original passage here then would have been: "Goddess brooded upon the face of the deep."

Thus, according to this one Bible scripture alone, Goddess truly did "create the Heaven and the Earth." (See GODDESS BLESS YOU; GODDESS THE CREATRESS; WORD OF GODDESS, THE)

GODDESSDAMN (the patriarchal form is: "goddamn")

This, the matriarchal form, is used as a noun or a verb, in place of the patriarchal version to condemn, criticize, or curse. Being an expletive that involves the holy name of the Supreme Being in its feminine aspect, this word is seldom used in its negative sense.

However, it does often occur (as does the patriarchal form) in more private or casual contexts, as well as in the religious ceremonies of Wiccens, and among white and black magic groups.

GODDESSDAMNED (the patriarchal form is: "goddamned")

This, the matriarchal form, is used as an adjective or

adverb, in place of the patriarchal version, to refer to the quality or state of being condemned or cursed.

Seldom, if ever, is this word used in sacred rituals since it is an expletive that employs the holy name of the Supreme Being in its feminine aspect. However, it does often occur (as does the patriarchal form) in more private or casual contexts.

GODDESSDAUGHTER (the patriarchal form is: "goddaughter")
This, the matriarchal form, is used as a noun, in place of the patriarchal version, indicating a female for whom another person becomes a sponsor at baptism.

GODDESSED (the patriarchal form is: "godded")
This, the matriarchal form, is used as a verb transitive, in place of the patriarchal version, meaning to treat as a goddess, or to idolize or deify.

GODDESS' ELECT (the patriarchal form is: "God's elect," a phrase long used by the Patriarchate, and commonly employed by biblical writers; see for example, Romans 8:33)
This, the matriarchal form, is used by Goddess-worshipers in place of the patriarchal version, to refer to those who have been accorded special dispensation by Goddess.

GODDESS ENRICHES (the patriarchal form is: "God enriches," the motto of Arizona)
In Arizona (and elsewhere), this, the matriarchal form, is

used by Goddess-worshipers in place of the patriarchal version.

GODDESSES WILLED OTHERWISE, THE (the patriarchal form is: "The gods willed otherwise," a popular expression taken from Virgil's *Aeneid*)

This, the matriarchal form, is used instead of the patriarchal version, to place responsibility for any failure on the will of the minor female deities.

GODDESSES WILL FIND A WAY, THE (the patriarchal form is: "The gods will find a way," an optimistic quote taken from Virgil's *Aeneid*)

This, the matriarchal form, is used by Goddess-worshipers in place of the patriarchal version.

GODDESSFATHER (the patriarchal form is: "godfather")

A noun indicating a man who sponsors a person at baptism. As a verb transitive, it refers to someone who acts as a goddessfather. Goddess-worshipers use this, the matriarchal form, in place of the patriarchal form.

GODDESS-FEARING (the patriarchal form is: "god-fearing")

This, the matriarchal form, is used by Goddess-worshipers in place of the patriarchal version, as an adjective meaning that one maintains a reverent or devoted feeling towards Goddess.

GODDESS FORBID (the patriarchal form is: "God forbid")

This, the matriarchal form, is used by Goddess-worshipers in place of the patriarchal version, as an exclamation of repugnance, hostility, or aversion.

GODDESSFORSAKEN (the patriarchal form is: "godforsaken")

This, the matriarchal form, is used by Goddess-worshipers in place of the patriarchal version, as an adjective referring either to something situated in a remote or desolate place, or to a miserable, dismal, or neglected person, place, or thing.

GODDESS HAS SMILED ON OUR ACCOMPLISHMENTS (the patriarchal form is: "He (God) has smiled on our accomplishments," a popular saying taken from Virgil's *Aeneid*)

This, the matriarchal form, is used by Goddess-worshipers in place of the patriarchal version. Interestingly, the patriarchal Latin form of this phrase, *Annuit Coeptis*, appears on the great seal of the U.S.A. (found on the back of our one-dollar bill). This fact is routinely touted by God-worshipers as evidence that "the U.S.A. was established on Christian values," under the auspices of the Old Testament Father-God Jehovah. The facts, however, tell a different story.

To begin with, many of the Founding Fathers were Masons and Deists, highly educated products of the 18th-Century Enlightenment. One, Thomas Jefferson, claimed no religious affiliation at all (as did two later presidents: Abraham Lincoln, a self-proclaimed "infidel," and Andrew Johnson). Another, George

Washington, the U.S.A.'s first president, remarked: "The government of the United States is not, in any sense, founded on the Christian religion."

From such facts it is clear that many of our Founders did not believe in "the Fall" or "Original Sin," and that as Masonic Deists *they viewed God as simply the sum total of the natural laws of the Universe*, rather than as an anthropomorphic deity with human-like attributes—the same basic view held by the Gnostic-oriented mystic, Saint John the Evangelist (see, for example, John 4:24).

In this sense these particular Founding Fathers would today probably be described by fundamentalist Christians as Atheists rather than Theists. Little wonder that Thomas Paine, the principle instigator of the idea of American independence from Britain, was later called a "filthy little atheist" by President Theodore Roosevelt (who did not seem to understand the precepts of Deism).

More to the point, the "sum total of the natural laws of the Universe" is simply another way of saying "Nature," a force, which long before the rise of the patriarchal monotheistic religions, was portrayed and venerated in feminine form as "Mother-Nature."

Additionally, the Latin of *Annuit Coeptis* is non-gender specific, which clearly means that the "God" whom the Founding Fathers believed had smiled on their accomplishments, need not have been male (that is, the Judeo-Christian Father-God called Yahweh or Jehovah). "She," or even "It," is equally applicable when interpreting this phrase.

But there are other clues that the U.S.A. was originally founded on the principles embodied in Goddess rather than in God.

We need merely glance at the Declaration of Independence (officially authorized on July 2, 1776) which, contrary to popular belief, nowhere contains any mention of the word "God." Indeed, the Declaration's primary architect, the non-religiously affiliated Jefferson, was careful to avoid the use of the word "God." Instead, being a Deist, he used ambiguous terms, part mystical, part scientific: "Creator," the "Supreme Judge," "Divine Providence," and the "Laws of Nature."

There is one reference to "Nature's God," but since Jefferson (who thoroughly repudiated organized religion) did not believe in the anthropomorphic male "God" of the Judeo-Christian heritage, he could not have been referring to this particular deity.

Again, the word "God" here was used by Jefferson as a gender-neutral, non-anthropomorphic reference to the universal "Laws of Nature," which for contemporary spiritual feminists is personified in the figure of Goddess.

There is other conspicuous evidence that the U.S.A. was founded on feminine not masculine principles.

Looking at the back side of the U.S. one-dollar bill, we find that the American eagle is clutching thirteen arrows in one claw, and a laurel branch with thirteen leaves in the other, while the flag shield on its chest contains thirteen stripes. Above the eagle's head is a star-burst containing thirteen stars (in the shape of a hexagram or "Star of David"), while the pyramid to the left contains thirteen different levels.

It is commonly assumed that these groups of "thirteen" symbolize the original thirteen colonies of the U.S.A., who declared their independence from Great Britain in 1776. While this would seem obvious at first glance, knowing what we do of the mystical beliefs of many of the Founding Fathers, we must seriously consider whether or not their use of this particular number was accidental or intentional.

For tens of thousands of years the number thirteen has been Goddess' most sacred number, since it correlates with her sacred Lunar Year, made up of exactly thirteen months, each possessing twenty-eight days, the number of days in a woman's menstrual cycle (the word "month," "menstruate," and "man," all derive from the word "Moon").

Even after the Patriarchal Takeover (around 4300 B.C.), when the thirteen-month Lunar Year was changed to the twelve-month Solar Year (in honor of the new patriarchalists' great Sun-God), Goddess continued to be portrayed as the Supreme Being surrounded by her twelve female Disciples, best known today in their masculinized forms as the "Twelve Sun-signs" of the Zodiac, or in worldwide mythology as, for example, the "Twelve Tribes of Israel," the "Twelve Knights of King Arthur's Round Table," the "Twelve Disciples of Buddha," the "Twelve Apostles of Jesus," the "Twelve Paladins of Roland," the "Twelve Labors of Hercules," and so on.

This form of Goddess as a solar-deity surrounded by twelve stars is wonderfully personified in the figure of the pre-Judeo-Christian Indian Goddess Aditi and her twelve Star-God Savior-Sons, the Adityas. The figure of Aditi was eventually borrowed by early Jewish mystics who penned the biblical book of Revelation.

Here the Pagan Goddess—whom modern Christians know as the "Virgin Mary"—appears in the New Testament as "a great wonder in heaven; a woman clothed with the sun, and the moon under her feet, and upon her head a crown of twelve stars" (Revelation 12:1).

Because it was so closely associated with Goddess, matriarchy, and feminine spirituality, the number thirteen fell into disfavor after the Patriarchal Takeover, In order to suppress the true meaning behind it, men forbade its use, imbued it with negative connotations, and labeled it an "evil number." To this day, many hotels and condominiums do not possess a thirteenth floor, Friday the Thirteenth is considered "bad luck," and we use the term "baker's dozen" in place of the word "thirteen."

And there is more.

The American eagle on the back of the one-dollar bill has nine tail feathers, and the star-burst above its head forms a nine-pointed hexagram when connected by lines. Nine, of course, is another one of Goddess' sacred numbers since it correlates with the nine-month gestation period of the human infant in the womb.

Is the appearance of the numbers nine and thirteen on U.S. currency a random fluke? Is it mere coincidence that a pyramid, an archetypal symbol of the female breast, figures so prominently on the one-dollar bill? Is it an accident that the pyramid has four sides, another sacred number of Goddess, representing the four seasons, the four elements (fire, earth, air, and water), and the "four corners of the Earth"—that is, Mother-Earth?

Is it mere chance that the American Founding Fathers, most of whom were learned in the occult arts, ancient (mainly Egyptian and Gnostic) symbolism, and the Goddess Religion, chose these specific feminine numbers and objects to decorate America's one-dollar bill?

Is it nothing more than serendipity that many of the Founders were Masons, a group that has long been associated with the Illuminati, an ancient secret Goddess-worshiping organization that has boasted such members as Leonardo da Vinci, whose famous artwork contains numerous allusions to the Divine Feminine?

We think not. (See IN GODDESS WE TRUST; SHE HAS FAVORED OUR UNDERTAKING)

GODDESSHEAD (the patriarchal form is: "godhead")

This, the matriarchal form, is used by Goddess-worshipers in place of the patriarchal version, as a noun indicating the essence or divinity of Goddess, either as a singular deity, or, in her form as the original Holy Trinity, an all-female pre-Christian deity known as the "Triple-Goddess." (See CRONE, MOTHER, AND VIRGIN-DAUGHTER)

GODDESS HELPS THOSE WHO HELP THEMSELVES (the patriarchal form is: "God helps those who help themselves")

This, the matriarchal form, is used by Goddess-worshipers in place of the patriarchal version.

Though this was one of Benjamin Franklin's more famous maxims, it comes originally from the 6th-Century B.C. Greek writer Aesop, who asserted that: "The gods help them that help themselves."

Long before Franklin, many others, including: Aeschylus, Sophocles, Euripides, and George Herbert, elaborated on Aesop's theme; always in the patriarchal form, however.

GODDESS HELP US (the patriarchal form is: "God help us")

This, the matricentric form, is used (either seriously or sarcastically) by Goddess-worshipers in place of the patriarchal version, to invoke the aid of the Supreme Being, Goddess.

GODDESS HELP YOU (the patriarchal form is: "God help you")

This, the matricentric form, is used (either seriously or sarcastically) by Goddess-worshipers in place of the patriarchal version, to invoke the aid of the Supreme Being, Goddess.

GODDESSHOOD (the patriarchal form is: "godhood")

This, the matricentric form, is used by Goddess-worshipers in place of the patriarchal version, as a noun indicating the Divinity as a feminine presence.

GODDESS' HOUSE (the patriarchal form is: "God's house," a phrase long used by the Patriarchy, and commonly employed by biblical writers; see for example, Genesis 28:22)

This, the matriarchal form, is used by Goddess-worshipers in place of the patriarchal version, in reference to a feminine place of worship (for instance, a forest, field, cave, synagogue, temple, pagoda, or church).

GODDESSING (the patriarchal form is: "godding")

This, the matriarchal form, is used in place of the patriarchal version, as a verb transitive meaning to treat one as a goddess; that is, to idolize or deify.

GODDESS KNOWS! (the patriarchal form is: "God knows!")

This, the matriarchal form, is used by Goddess-worshipers in place of the patriarchal version, to begin a statement or sentence, or as a reply to a question.

GODDESS' LAW (the patriarchal form is: "God's law," a phrase long used by the Patriarchy, and commonly employed by biblical writers; see for example, Nehemiah 10:29)

This, the matriarchal form, is used by Goddess-worshipers in place of the patriarchal version, to refer to the principles and edicts of Goddess.

GODDESSLESS (the patriarchal form is: "godless")

This, the matriarchal form, is used by Goddess-worshipers in place of the patriarchal version, as an adjective referring to the state or quality in which Goddess and her Divine Laws are not acknowledged or revered.

GODDESSLESSNESS (the patriarchal form is: "godlessness")

This, the matriarchal form, is used by Goddess-worshipers in place of the patriarchal version, as a noun indicating the state or quality of being goddessless or atheistic.

GODDESSLIKE (the patriarchal form is: "godlike")

    This, the matriarchal form, is used by Goddess-worshipers in place of the patriarchal version, as either an adjective describing the quality of resembling Goddess, or as the state of possessing the qualities of Goddess or of a goddess.

GODDESSLIKENESS (the patriarchal form is: "godlikeness")

    This, the matriarchal form, is used by Goddess-worshipers in place of the patriarchal version, as a noun indicating the state or quality of bearing a resemblance to Goddess or to a goddess.

GODDESSLING (the patriarchal form is: "godling")

    This, the matriarchal form, is used by Goddess-worshipers in place of the patriarchal version, as a noun indicating a minor, local, or sometimes inferior female deity.

GODDESSLIER (the patriarchal form is: "godlier")

    This, the matriarchal form, is used by Goddess-worshipers in place of the patriarchal version, as an adjective to indicate the state or quality of being more divine, pious, or devout than others.

GODDESSLIEST (the patriarchal form is: "godliest")

    This, the matriarchal form, is utilized by Goddess-worshipers in place of the patriarchal version, as an adjective meant to describe the quality or state of being most like Goddess, or the most devout.

GODDESSLINESS (the patriarchal form is: "godliness")

This, the matriarchal form, is utilized by Goddess-worshipers in place of the patriarchal version, as a noun meant to indicate the state or quality of possessing the divine qualities of Goddess or of a goddess.

GODDESSLY (the patriarchal form is: "godly")

This, the matriarchal form, is used by Goddess-worshipers in place of the patriarchal version, as an adjective or an adverb to describe the state, or apparent state, or quality of being divine, pious, or devout.

GODDESS MADE THE COUNTRY, WOMAN MADE THE TOWN (the patriarchal form is: "God made the country, man made the town," a humanistic maxim penned by the 1st-Century B.C. Roman scholar, Marcus Terentius Varro)

This, the matriarchal form, is used by Goddess-worshipers in place of the patriarchal version, in matriotic honor of Goddess, women, and the Feminine Principle.

GODDESS-MOTHER (the patriarchal form is: "god-mother")

This, the matriarchal form, is used by Goddess-worshipers in place of the patriarchal version, as a noun that indicates a woman who sponsors a person at baptism.

GODDESSPARENT (the patriarchal form is: "godparent")

This, the matriarchal form, is used by Goddess-worshipers

in place of the patriarchal version, as a noun indicating someone who acts as a sponsor at a baptism.

GODDESS' PRIESTESSES (the patriarchal form is: "God's ministers," a phrase long used by the Patriarchy, and commonly employed by biblical writers; see for example, Romans 13:6)

This, the matriarchal form, is used by Goddess-worshipers in place of the patriarchal version, to refer to those women who work under the auspices of the Great Mother, Goddess.

GODDESS' RIGHTEOUSNESS (the patriarchal form is: "God's righteousness," a phrase long used by the Patriarchy, and commonly employed by biblical writers; see for example, Romans 10:3)

This, the matriarchal form, is used by Goddess-worshipers in place of the patriarchal version, to denote the justness and virtuousness of Goddess.

GODDESS SAVE THE KING (the patriarchal form is: "God Save the King")

This, the matriarchal form, is used by Goddess-worshipers in place of the patriarchal version, as a salutation, toast, or prayer.

GODDESS SAVE THE QUEEN (the patriarchal form is: "God Save the Queen")

This, the matriarchal form, is used by Goddess-worshipers in place of the patriarchal version, as a salutation, toast, or prayer.

GODDESSSEND (the patriarchal form is: "godsend")

This, the matriarchal form, is used by Goddess-worshipers in place of the patriarchal version, as a noun indicating a desirable, or needed thing, or an event that comes unexpectedly—courtesy of Goddess.

GODDESS-SENT (the patriarchal form is: "god-sent")

This, the matriarchal form, is used by Goddess-worshipers in place of the patriarchal version, as an adjective that describes something that appears at a fortuitous time, as if by the Divine Will of Goddess.

GODDESSSON (the patriarchal form is: "godson")

This, the matriarchal form, is used by Goddess-worshipers in place of the patriarchal version, as a noun indicating a male goddesschild. (See GODDESSCHILD)

GODDESSSPEED (the patriarchal form is: "godspeed")

This, the matriarchal form, is used by Goddess-worshipers in place of the patriarchal version, as a noun deriving from the 16th-Century English phrase: "Goddess spede you," that is, "Goddess prosper you." The hopeful implication here is that one will have a successful journey or undertaking with the aid of Goddess.

GODDESS THE CREATRESS (the patriarchal form is: "God the Creator," a phrase long used by the Patriarchy, and commonly employed by biblical writers; see for example, Isaiah 40:28;

Romans 1:25)

This, the matriarchal form, is used by Goddess-worshipers in place of the patriarchal version. The world's earliest creation legends depict a female deity, a Great Creatrix, generating the Universe, the stars, the Earth, and life. The idea that a male deity could be procreative was unthinkable in ancient times, since the biological knowledge of paternity was entirely unknown.

After the Patriarchal Takeover (c. 4300 B.C.), however, the priests and mythographers of the new androcentric religions sought to eradicate all vestiges of matriarchy, which included the idea of a female Supreme Being.

One aspect of this entailed appropriating the Goddess Creation Legends. In the process, Goddess the Creatress was masculinized, becoming "God the Creator." This phrase was then inserted into the Patriarchy's Creation Myth, which was then spread around the world in an attempt to supplant the far older female-based Creation Myth. This explains the incongruity of the Judeo-Christian Father-God (Yahweh-Jehovah) "giving birth" to the Cosmos, the world, and all life (see Genesis 1:1-31; 2:1-3).

Despite this overt plagiarism, thousands of pre-Judeo-Christian myths record the existence of a universal feminine Creatress, a testimony to the once great Sisterhood, or global Matriarchate, and the worldwide Religion of Goddess, at whose head Goddess herself stood for hundreds of thousands of years.

The following are just a few of the many hundreds of thousands of the world's Creatresses:

- ▼ Aditi (India)
- ▼ Ararat (Anatolia/Armenia)
- ▼ Asherah (Semitic: Judaism)
- ▼ Ataensic (North America: Iroquois)
- ▼ Atse Estsan (North America: Navaho)
- ▼ Bhavani (India)
- ▼ Cally Berry (Ireland)
- ▼ Cerridwen (Wales)
- ▼ Cipactli (Mexico)
- ▼ Coatlicue (Mexico)
- ▼ Danu (Ireland)
- ▼ Devi (India)
- ▼ Eingana (Australia)
- ▼ Eriu (Ireland)
- ▼ Eve (Semitic: Judeo-Christian)
- ▼ Frigga (Scandinavia)
- ▼ Ganga (India)
- ▼ Hera (Greece)
- ▼ Hina (Polynesia)
- ▼ Ila (India)
- ▼ Inanna (Sumeria)
- ▼ Ishtar (Babylonia)
- ▼ Isis (Egypt)
- ▼ Isong (Africa: Ibibio and Ekoi)
- ▼ Izanami (Japan)
- ▼ Kadru (India)
- ▼ Kali (India)

- ▼ Khon-Ma (Tibet)
- ▼ Koevasi (Melanesia)
- ▼ Kottavi (India)
- ▼ Kuma (Venezuela)
- ▼ Lla-Mo (Tibet)
- ▼ Mawu (Africa: Dahomey)
- ▼ Mokosh (Slavonia)
- ▼ Muk Jauk (Cambodia)
- ▼ Nemesis (Greece)
- ▼ Obatallah (Brazil)
- ▼ Omamama (North America: Cree)
- ▼ Pheraia (Greek)
- ▼ Po Ino Nogar (Cambodia)
- ▼ Qamaits (North America: Bellacoola)
- ▼ Rhea (Italy)
- ▼ Sarah (Semitic: Judeo-Christian)
- ▼ Sarasvati (India)
- ▼ Sedna (North America: Eskimo)
- ▼ Sela (Africa: Luhya)
- ▼ Shiwanokia (North America: Zuni)
- ▼ Tabiti (Scythia)
- ▼ Tanith (Carthage)
- ▼ Tethys (Greece)
- ▼ Thetis (Greece)
- ▼ Tiamat (Babylonia)
- ▼ Tundr Ilona (Hungary)
- ▼ Uti Hiata (North America: Pawnee)

▼ Vut-Imi (Siberia)
▼ Waramurungundji (Australia)
▼ White Buffalo Woman (North America: Oglala)
▼ Yebaad (North America: Navaho)
▼ Zywie (Poland)

(See GODDESS; GODDESS CREATED THE HEAVEN AND THE EARTH; HEAVENLY MOTHER; MOTHER)

GODDESS THE MOTHER (the patriarchal form is: "God the Father," a phrase long used by the Patriarchy, and commonly employed by biblical writers; see for example, Galatians 1:1)

This, the matriarchal form, is used by Goddess-worshipers in place of the patriarchal version, to denote the great maternal deity, Goddess. (See GODDESS; HEAVENLY MOTHER: MOTHER)

GODDESS' THRONE (the patriarchal form is: "God's throne," a phrase long used by the Patriarchy, and commonly employed by biblical writers; see for example, Matthew 5:34)

This, the matriarchal form, is used by Goddess-worshipers in place of the patriarchal version, as an allusion to Goddess' awesome spiritual power.

GODDESS' TRUTH, THE (the patriarchal form is: "the God's truth")

This, the matriarchal form, is used by Goddess-worshipers

in place of the patriarchal version, to denote a fact or reality that has the power of Goddess behind it.

GODDESS' WIFERY (the patriarchal form is: "God's husbandry," a phrase long used by the Patriarchy, and commonly employed by biblical writers; see for example, 1 Corinthians 3:9)

This, the matriarchal form, is used by Goddess-worshipers in place of the patriarchal version, in reference to Goddess' works.

GODDESS' WILL (the patriarchal form is: "God's will")

An ancient phrase used to express the fatalism of entrusting life to the feminine Supreme Being. This, the matriarchal form, is used by Goddess-worshipers in place of the patriarchal version.

GODDESS WILL GRANT AN END EVEN TO THESE (TROUBLES) (the patriarchal form is: "God will grant an end even to these (troubles)," a saying taken from Virgil's *Aeneid*)

This, the matriarchal form, is used by Goddess-worshipers in place of the patriarchal version, as an optimistic invocation of Goddess' beneficence.

GODDESS WILLING (the patriarchal form is: "God willing")

An ancient expression used to enlist the aid of the feminine Supreme Being in an enterprise. This, the matriarchal form, is used by Goddess-worshipers in place of the patriarchal version.

GODDESS WILLS IT (the patriarchal form is: "God wills it," the 11th-Century battle cry of the Christians of the 1st Crusade)

This, the matriarchal form, is used by Goddess-worshipers in place of the patriarchal version, to signify that Goddess' unyielding resolve lies behind a particular belief or action.

GODDESSWIT (the patriarchal form is: "godwit")

This, the matriarchal form, is used by Goddess-worshipers in place of the patriarchal version, as a noun indicating those long-billed wading birds of the genus *Limosa*, who are related to the snipes, but which resemble curlews.

GOODDESS (the patriarchal form is: "good")

This, the matriarchal form, is used by Goddess-worshipers in place of the patriarchal version, as an inflation derived from the noun "goddess," just as the word "good" is an inflation of the noun "god." (The Norwegian word for "good," for example, is *god*.)

The word gooddess may be used as an adjective, a noun, or an adverb, to describe or indicate something of a favorable tendency, or someone of a favorable character.

GOODDESSISH (the patriarchal form is: "goodish")

An adjective describing the quality or state of being potentially positive or benevolent. Goddess-worshipers use this, the matriarchal form, in place of the patriarchal form. (See GOODDESS)

GOODDESS BOOK, THE (the patriarchal form is: "the good book")

 This, the matriarchal form, is used by Goddess-worshipers in place of the patriarchal version, as a 19th-Century noun-phrase indicating the Judeo-Christian holy book, the Bible, a monument to the Patriarchy, and a chronicle of the Judeo-Christian Patriarchal Takeover of Goddess and the Goddess World. (See GOODDESS; GODDESS)

GOODDESS-BYE (the patriarchal form is: "good-bye")

 This, the matriarchal form, is used by Goddess-worshipers in place of the patriarchal version, as a farewell, concluding remark, or gesture at parting company.

 The noun "gooddess-bye" is a corrupted English derivation of the ancient phrase "Goddess be with ye." Britain, like all early cultures, was a Goddess-worshiping nation (as I show in my book *Britannia Rules*). Indeed, Britain derives it name from the great Celtic Triple-Goddess Brigantia (in Scotland she is known as Bride; in Ireland, Brigid; in France, Brigandu), whom the Romans called Britannia, an all-powerful female deity later trivialized, marginalized, and Christianized as "Saint Bridget." (See GOODDESS)

GOODDESS FAITH (the patriarchal form is: "good faith")

 This, the matriarchal form, is used by Goddess-worshipers in place of the patriarchal version, as a noun-phrase indicating a quality of honesty or lawfulness of purpose. (See GOODDESS)

GOODDESS-FELLOW (the patriarchal form is: "good-fellow")

This, the matriarchal form, is used by Goddess-worshipers in place of the patriarchal version, as a noun indicating an affable and companionable person. (See GOODDESS)

GOODDESS-FELLOWSHIP (the patriarchal form is: "good-fellowship")

This, the matriarchal form, is used by Goddess-worshipers in place of the patriarchal version, as a noun indicating a quality or state of companionship, partnership, or community of interest. (See GOODDESS)

GOODDESS FRIDAY (the patriarchal form is: "Good Friday")

This, the matriarchal form, is used by Goddess-worshipers in place of the patriarchal version, as a noun-phrase indicating the Friday before Easter, observed in orthodox patriarchal Christianity as the anniversary of the crucifixion of its Sun-God (now spelled, as I discuss in my book *Christmas Before Christianity*, "Son-God"), Jesus. And for good reason. Long prior to the rise of Christianity the sixth day of the week was, for thousands of years, ruled over by Goddess in her form as a love-deity.

Indeed, the word Friday comes from the name of the Scandinavian Sex-Goddess variously called Fri, Frig, Frigga, or Freya. In Old English Friday was written *Frigedæg*, meaning "Frig's Day." The American slang words frig and frigging ("masturbate") both derive from the Goddess Frigga. The Romans gave Friday the name *Dies Veneris* ("Day of Venus") after Venus, their own version of the great Sex-Goddess. Hence, in modern French and Italian Friday is still spelled *Vendredi* and *Venerdì*, respectively.

Due to the "fishy" smell of the magical life-bearing female genitalia, one of Venus' totemic animals is the fish, which is why in ancient times fish were eaten on her sacred day, Friday—a ritual meant to promote fertility. Ever since, the fish has been considered an aphrodisiac, a word derived from the name of the Greek version of the European Sex-Goddess, Aphrodite.

Friday the Thirteenth was considered a particularly propitious day for ensuring fecundity, since the number thirteen is one of Goddess' most sacred numbers: Goddess' 364-day Holy Lunar Year (based on the passage of the Moon rather than of the Sun) has thirteen months, each comprised of four seven-day weeks equaling twenty-eight days, the number of days in a woman's menstrual cycle. Though it no longer fits precisely into the Patriarchate's 365-day Solar Year system, our seven-day week is a vestige of the first calendric year, the once worldwide Lunar Year of Goddess, invented by prehistoric women in an effort to keep track of their menses.

When orthodox Christianity (originally the Catholic Church) began taking over the myths, figures, words, customs, rituals, holy days, and clothing of Paganism in the early Medieval period, they adopted the Goddess custom of eating fish on Friday. (Since many of the first orthodox Christians were Pagan converts who were loathe to give up their beloved habits, the Church had little choice but to adopt Pagan customs if it wanted to retain and strengthen its membership.)

To this day, however, the Church does not discuss the matriarchal origins of the practice of eating fish on Friday. Instead, the Patriarchy has demonized Goddess and everything that is sacred to her. In this way Friday the Thirteenth became "unlucky," while Friday itself came to be known in Christianity as "the day of Devil worship."

In addition, Friday evening continues to be considered "date night" among teenagers, who unknowingly carry on the ancient Pagan tradition of focusing on physical intimacy on the sixth day of the week in honor of the Pagan Love- and Sex-Goddess.

Later, Venus-Aphrodite was desexualized and Christianized as Jesus' mother, the Virgin Mary, to whom was appended the symbol called the Vesica Pisces, meaning "fish bladder," or more loosely, "Vessel of the Fish." The "fish" inside the "vessel" is Jesus, the "fisher of men" who was born out of Mary's sacred womb, known as the Mandorla, created by the intersection of the two circles that make up the Vesica Pisces emblem. The resulting almond-shaped symbol (*mandorla* is Italian for "little almond") is vulva-shaped, and thus mystically corresponds to the entrance of the "womb of the Great Goddess, Mother of the Universe and All Life."

Naturally, the Pagan Mandorla found its way into Christian iconography: not only have Mary and Jesus long been artistically portrayed *inside* both the Vesica Pisces and the Mandorla, but many European churches and cathedrals sport a figure known as the Sheela Na Gig, a crude stone carving of a naked female displaying exaggerated pudenda, yet another remnant of the prehistoric Pagan

Goddess religion that has been adopted by Christianity. Mary is still known by the ancient Pagan Goddess title Stella Maris ("Star of the Sea")—also a Medieval name for the North Star. (See GODDESS; GOODDESS)

GOODDESS GODDESS! (the patriarchal form is: "good God!")
This, the matriarchal form, is used by Goddess-worshipers in place of the patriarchal version. In this exclamatory phrase, we have the technically correct spelling of "good goddess." (See GOODDESS)

GOODDESS-HEARTED (the patriarchal form is: "good-hearted")
This, the matriarchal form, is used by Goddess-worshipers in place of the patriarchal version, as an adjective describing the quality or state of being kindly and generous. (See GOODDESS)

GOODDESS-HEARTEDLY (the patriarchal form is: "good-heartedly")
This, the matriarchal form, is used by Goddess-worshipers in place of the patriarchal version, as an adverb describing an action performed with a quality of generosity. (See GOODDESS)

GOODDESS-HEARTEDNESS (the patriarchal form is: "good-heartedness")
This, the matriarchal form, is used by Goddess-worshipers in place of the patriarchal version, as a noun indicating a quality or state of altruism, humanitarianism, and benevolence. (See

GOODDESS)

GOODDESS-HUMORED (the patriarchal form is: "good-humored")

    An adjective describing the state or quality of being cheerful and accommodating. Goddess-worshipers use this, the matriarchal form, in place of the patriarchal version. (See GOODDESS)

GOODDESS-HUMOREDLY (the patriarchal form is: "good-humoredly")

    An adverb describing an action performed with a quality of cheerfulness. Goddess-worshipers use this, the matriarchal form, in place of the patriarchal version. (See GOODDESS)

GOODDESS-HUMOREDNESS (the patriarchal form is: "good-humoredness")

    A noun indicating a quality or state of optimism and joy. Goddess-worshipers use this, the matriarchal form, in place of the patriarchal version. (See GOODDESS)

GOODDESS LIFE, THE (the patriarchal form is: "the good life")

    This, the matriarchal form, is used by Goddess-worshipers in place of the patriarchal version, as a noun-phrase indicating the quality of a life marked by a comfortable or high standard of living. (See GOODDESS)

GOODDESS-LOOKER (the patriarchal form is: "good-looker")

 This, the matriarchal form, is used by Goddess-worshipers in place of the patriarchal version, as a noun indicating the state or quality of being particularly attractive, beautiful, or handsome. (See GOODDESS)

GOODDESS-LOOKING (the patriarchal form is: "good-looking")

 This, the matriarchal form, is used by Goddess-worshipers in place of the patriarchal version, as an adjective describing the quality or state of being attractive, or of having a pleasant appearance. (See GOODDESS)

GOODDESSLADY (the patriarchal form is: "goodlady")

 This, the matriarchal form, is used by Goddess-worshipers in place of the patriarchal version, as a noun indicating the female head of a household. (See GOODDESS)

GOODDESSLY (the patriarchal form is: "goodly")

 This, the matriarchal form, is used in place of the patriarchal version, as an adjective describing the quality or state of being pleasantly attractive or significantly large.

GOODDESSLIER (the patriarchal form is: "goodlier")

 This, the matriarchal form, is used by Goddess-worshipers in place of the patriarchal version, as an adjective describing the quality or state of being more pleasant or attractive, or larger, than something or someone else. (See GOODDESS)

GOODDESSLIEST (the patriarchal form is: "goodliest")

An adjective describing the quality or state of being the most pleasant, attractive, or large. Goddess-worshipers use this, the matriarchal form, in place of the patriarchal version. (See GOODDESS)

GOODDESSMAN (the patriarchal form is: "goodman")

This, the matriarchal form, is used by Goddess-worshipers in place of the patriarchal version, as a noun indicating the male head of a household. (See GOODDESS)

GOODDESS-NATURED (the patriarchal form is: "good-natured")

This, the matriarchal form, is used by Goddess-worshipers in place of the patriarchal version, as an adjective describing the quality or state of being pleasant, cheerful, and cooperative. (See GOODDESS)

GOODDESS-NATUREDLY (the patriarchal form is: "good-naturedly")

This, the matriarchal form, is used by Goddess-worshipers in place of the patriarchal version, as an adverb describing the quality or state of an amiable action. (See GOODDESS)

GOODDESS-NATUREDNESS (the patriarchal form is: "good-naturedness")

This, the matriarchal form, is used by Goddess-worshipers

in place of the patriarchal version, as a noun indicating the quality or state of being agreeable or cooperative. (See GOODDESS)

GOODDESS-NEIGHBOR (the patriarchal form is: "good-neighbor")
     This, the matriarchal form, is used by Goddess-worshipers in place of the patriarchal version, as an adjective describing the principles of friendship, cooperation, and noninterference. (See GOODDESS)

GOODDESSNESS (the patriarchal form is: "goodness")
     This, the matriarchal form, is used by Goddess-worshipers in place of the patriarchal version, as a noun indicating the state or quality of being good, or rather gooddess, or beneficial. (See GOODDESS)

GOODDESS-TEMPERED (the patriarchal form is: "good-tempered")
     This, the matriarchal form, is used by Goddess-worshipers in place of the patriarchal version, as an adjective describing the quality of being patient and amiable. (See GOODDESS)

GOODDESS-TEMPEREDLY (the patriarchal form is: "good-temperedly")
     This, the matriarchal form, is used by Goddess-worshipers in place of the patriarchal version, as an adverb describing the quality of being composed. (See GOODDESS

GOODDESS-TEMPEREDNESS (the patriarchal form is: "good-temperedness")

    This, the matriarchal form, is used by Goddess-worshipers in place of the patriarchal version, as a noun indicating the quality or state of being stable. (See GOODDESS)

GOODDESS-WIFE (the patriarchal form is: "good-wife")

    This, the matriarchal form, is used by Goddess-worshipers in place of the patriarchal version, as a 13th-Century noun indicating the mistress or lady of the house. Archaically employed as we now use "Mrs." or "Ms." (See GOODDESS)

GOODDESSWILL (the patriarchal form is: "goodwill")

    This, the matriarchal form, is used in place of the patriarchal version, as a noun indicating a kindly feeling of support or approval. (See GOODDESS)

GOODDESSWILLED (the patriarchal form is: "goodwilled")

    This, the matriarchal form, is used by Goddess-worshipers in place of the patriarchal version, as an adjective describing the quality of having a charitable spirit. (See GOODDESS)

GOODDESSIE (the patriarchal form is: "goodie")

    This, the matriarchal form, is used by Goddess-worshipers in place of the patriarchal version, as a noun indicating the quality or state of being particularly attractive, pleasurable, or desirable. (See GOODDESS)

GOODDESSY (the patriarchal form is: "goody")

This, the matriarchal form, is used by Goddess-worshipers in place of the patriarchal version. Gooddessy is a corruption of the noun "gooddesswife" (the patriarchal version is "goodwife") which, in the Medieval period, indicated a married woman of lowly station. (See GOODDESS; GOODESS-WIFE)

GOOD GODDESS (the patriarchal form is: "good God")

This, the matriarchal form, is used by Goddess-worshipers in place of the patriarchal version. Technically, the correct spelling is "gooddess Goddess." (See GOODDESS)

Votive relief of Aphrodite and Aries.

The Virgin Mary artistically portrayed inside the Vesica Pisces or Mandorla.

Jesus pictured inside the almond-shaped Vesica Pisces or Mandorla.

One of the Evangelists drawn inside the Vesica Pisces or Mandorla.

Another portrait of the Virgin Mary inside the Vesica Pisces or Mandorla.

HEAVENLY MOTHER (the patriarchal form is: "Heavenly Father," an ancient universal title of the archetypal Father-God, known variously across the world as: Brahma, Zeus, Jupiter, Yahweh, Ra, Baal, Amma, El, Odin, Osiris, Jehovah, Anu, Saturn, Jesus, Bran, Adad, Enlil, Martu, Woden, or simply God. The title "Heavenly Father" was often employed by biblical writers; see for example, Matthew 15:13. The name of the Roman father-god, Jupiter (Iu-Pater), is a Latinization of the older Indian father-god, called, in Sanskrit, *Dyaus Pitar,* a word-title which itself means "Divine Father," or more loosely, "Heavenly-Father." Among the ancient Egyptians the Latin word Iu-Pater became Ieu, among the Greeks it became Iason (that is, Jason), while among the early Jews, it became Yahu, Jahi, Yahweh, Yehowshuwa, or Yeshua (that is, Joshua). Borrowing on the motif of the universal father-god, early Medieval Greek-speaking orthodox Christians called their own paternal deity Jehovah or Iesous, while among Latin-speaking Christians he came to be referred to as Jesus).

This, the matriarchal form, is used by Goddess-worshippers in place of the patriarchal version, when speaking of, or addressing, Goddess.

Throughout history "Heavenly Mother" has been the most popular title of Goddess and the minor goddesses, particularly the mother-goddesses, which is why it was usurped by the Patriarchy, masculinized, and given to the new Father-God.

Among the thousands of goddesses who have been given this title, we have: Juno, Ishtar, Astarte, Asherah, Isis, and Ashteroth. Orthodox Christians later appended the title to their own version of the Great Mother-Goddess, the Virgin Mary.

Besides Heavenly Mother, Goddess' other most popular title is "Queen of Heaven," another Pagan appellation that was later stolen and appended to the Virgin Mary (see for example, Jeremiah 7:18; 44:17-19; 44:25). (See GODDESS; MOTHER)

HEAVENS BESPEAK THE GLORY OF GODDESS, THE (the patriarchal form is: "the heavens bespeak the glory of God," a quote from the book of Psalms 19:1)

This, the matriarchal form, is used by Goddess-worshipers in place of the patriarchal version, as a favorable comment on the debut of a new public figure.

HONEST TO GODDESS (the patriarchal form is: "honest to God")

This, the matriarchal form, is used by Goddess-worshipers in place of the patriarchal version, as a phrase denoting an oath or statement of great sincerity invoked in the name of Goddess.

HOWSOEVER IT SHALL PLEASE GODDESS (the patriarchal form is: "howsoever it shall please God")

This, the matriarchal form, is used by Goddess-worshipers

in place of the patriarchal version, as an ancient phrase used in invocations to Goddess.

Head of the "Crouching Venus."

Cnidian Venus of Praxiteles, Vatican Museum, Rome.

I

I AM THE LADY YOUR GODDESS (the patriarchal form is: "I am the Lord your God," a phrase long used by the Patriarchate, and commonly employed by biblical writers; see for example, Leviticus 19:25)

This, the matriarchal form, is used by Goddess-worshipers in place of the patriarchal version, in feministic writings, myths, stories, and rituals.

IF GODDESS WILLS IT (the patriarchal form is: "If God wills it")

This, the matriarchal form, is used by Goddess-worshipers in place of the patriarchal version, as an ancient expression of resignation and perhaps pessimism.

IF IT PLEASE THE GODDESSES (the patriarchal form is: "If it please the gods")

This, the matriarchal form, is used by Goddess-worshipers in place of the patriarchal version, as an ancient expression meaning to surrender to fate.

IN GODDESS WE TRUST (the patriarchal form is: "In God We Trust" the motto inscribed on the currency of the U.S.A.)

This, the matriarchal form, is used by Goddess-worshipers

in place of the patriarchal version, to indicate that one is placing one's destiny in the hands of Goddess. (See GODDESS HAS SMILED ON OUR ACCOMPLISHMENTS.)

IN THE NAME OF GODDESS (the patriarchal form is: "In the name of God")

This, the matriarchal form, is used by Goddess-worshipers in place of the patriarchal version, as an ancient expression utilized in religious ceremonies and at other times in an informal context.

IN THE YEAR OF OUR LADY (the patriarchal form is: "In the year of our Lord")

This, the matriarchal form, is used by Goddess-worshipers in place of the patriarchal version, to specify a time period that takes place under the auspices of Our Lady, Goddess.

The patriarchal phrase "in the year of our Lord" derives from the early Christian custom of correlating the beginning of the Christian era with the birth of Christianity's Sun-God, Jesus. To the present day the Western calender is reckoned upon this date; that is, 0 A.D.

In Latin, "in the year of our Lord" is written *Anno Domini* (which gives us the modern acronym A.D.). However, since the Latin word for "lady" is *domina*, the expression *Anno Domina* could just as easily be used—since the first calenders were invented by women.

Most contemporary scientists and scholars have done away with the usage of A.D. altogether, replacing it with the more neutral C.E., meaning the "Common Era," which began in the year 0. When dealing with time periods prior to the beginning of the Common Era, B.C.E. is thus used, an acronym for "Before the Common Era." (As a mystical Christian I have retained the traditional abbreviations.)

It would certainly be appropriate for Goddess-worshipers to create a calender based on the birthday of the feminine Supreme Being rather than on the male one. However, this would be difficult, for unlike the patriarchal Father-God, Goddess does not have a birthday. Why? Because she is, in fact, immortal; she has always existed and always will.

It is true that many of the minor goddesses do have sacred days and holy feast days. For example, the feast day of the Celtic Goddess Brigid is February 2; the feast day of the Roman Goddess Juno is March 1; the feast day of the Greek Goddess Maia is May 1 ("May Day"); the feast day of the Slavic Goddess Ursala is October 21; and the feast day of the Babylonian Goddess Nanshe is January 1. However, the *year* in which these goddesses were born is unknown, making the development of a calender around them impossible.

There is one alternative for those in the Christianized West. Here, Goddess-worshipers could initiate a female-based calender around the birth date of the Christian version of Goddess: the Virgin Mary who, according to Christian mythology, was born on September 8 and was twelve years old when she gave birth to Jesus. The modern Western Goddess calender then would begin on September 8 in what is now the year 12 B.C. Thus, under the new

Goddess calender our current God year, 1997 *Anno Domini* (A.D.), would become the Goddess year 1985 *Anno Domina* (A.D.): "the year of our Lady."

In other words, the Goddess year adds twelve years to our current (God-oriented, male-biased) Gregorian calender—twelve being the sacred number of the Zodiac, which has been variously mythologized as the Twelve Knights of King Arthur, the Twelve Paladins of Roland, the Twelves Tribes of Isis-Ra-El (that is, Israel), the Twelve Labors of Hercules, the Twelve Disciples of Buddha, the Twelve Apostles of Jesus. (See GODDESS HAS SMILED ON OUR ACCOMPLISHMENTS)

Isis, the Egyptian Virgin Mother-Goddess with the universal totemic female fish symbol.

I THE LADY YOUR GODDESS AM HOLY (the patriarchal form is: "I the Lord your God am holy," a phrase long used by the Patriarchy, and commonly employed by biblical writers; see for example, Leviticus 19:2)

This, the matriarchal form, is used by Goddess-worshipers in place of the patriarchal version, in feminine sacred writings and religious rituals.

L

LADY, DIRECT US (the patriarchal form is: "Lord, direct us," the motto of London, England)

This, the matriarchal form, is used by Goddess-worshipers, British ones in particular, in place of the patriarchal version, as an appeal to the Supreme Being, Goddess, for guidance.

LADY GODDESS (the patriarchal form is: "Lord God")

This, the matriarchal form, is a title used by Goddess-worshipers in place of the patriarchal version, when referring to or addressing the Supreme Being, Goddess.

LADY GODDESS OF THEIR MOTHERS, THE (the patriarchal form is: "the Lord God of their fathers," a phrase long used by the Patriarchy, and commonly employed by biblical writers; see for example, Exodus 4:5)

This, the matriarchal form, is a title used by Goddess-worshipers in place of the patriarchal version, when referring to the Supreme Being, Goddess.

LADY IS MY LIGHT, THE (the patriarchal form is: "The Lord is my light," the motto of England's Oxford University)

This, the matriarchal form, is used by Oxfordian Goddess-worshipers, and others, in place of the patriarchal version, in female-based writings and rites.

LADY HAVE MERCY (the patriarchal form is: "Lord have mercy," a phrase long used by the Patriarchy, and commonly employed by biblical writers; see for example, Matthew 17:15; 20:30-31)

This, the matriarchal form, is used by Goddess-worshipers in place of the patriarchal version, as an appeal for clemency and sympathy from the Great Mother: Goddess.

LADY'S PRAYER, THE (the patriarchal form is: "the Lord's Prayer," the patriarchal version found in the Judeo-Christian holy book, the Bible; see Matthew 6:9; Luke 11:2)

This, the matriarchal form, is used by Goddess-worshipers in place of the patriarchal version. Women have reclaimed the original matriarchal benediction to Goddess and given it its proper name, "The Lady's Prayer." It now once again reads:

> Our Mother which art in heaven, Hallowed by thy name. Thy Queendom come. Thy will be done in earth, as it is in heaven. Give us this day our daily bread. And forgive us our debts, as we forgive our debtors. And lead us not into temptation, but deliver us from evil: For thine is the Queendom, and the power, and the glory, forever. Awomyn.

LADY OUR GODDESS, THE (the patriarchal form is: "the Lord our God," a phrase long used by the Patriarchy, and commonly employed by biblical writers; see for example, Exodus 5:3)

This, the matriarchal form, is a title used by Goddess-worshipers in place of the patriarchal version, when referring to the Supreme Being: Goddess.

LADY THY GODDESS IS A JEALOUS GODDESS, THE (the patriarchal form is: "the Lord thy God is a jealous God," a phrase long used by the Patriarchy, and commonly employed by biblical writers; see for example, Exodus 20:5)

This, the matriarchal form, is used by Goddess-worshipers in place of the patriarchal version, in reference to Goddess' desire that her children honor her name and her principles only.

LAMB OF GODDESS (the patriarchal form is: "Lamb of God," a title applied to Jesus by John the Baptist; see John 1:29, 36)

This, the matriarchal form, is used by Goddess-worshipers in place of the patriarchal version, to denote that all saviors, messiahs, and christs—male *and* female—are born of women, the veritable "Daughters of Goddess."

LEAVE THE REST TO THE GODDESSES (the patriarchal form is: "Leave the rest to the gods," a pragmatic, cynical expression from Horace's *Odes*)

This, the matriarchal form, is used by Goddess-worshipers in place of the patriarchal version, as an expression of resignation.

Aphrodite with a rabbit, a female fecundity symbol.

Attic goddess sculpture (two views) from the 5th Century B.C.

Post Patriarchal Takeover: The patriarchal nuclear family, now comprised of a father, mother, and children. This replaced the matriarchal nuclear family, which consisted of a mother and her children (the same family structure still found in most mammal species).

MAY GODDESS HAVE MERCY (the patriarchal form is: "May God have mercy," a quote taken from the patriarchal book of Psalms 6:2; 9:13)

This, the matriarchal form, is used by Goddess-worshipers in place of the patriarchal version. This ancient expression invokes the cooperation of the feminine Supreme Being in various acts and endeavors.

MOTHER (the patriarchal form is: "Father," a title of the Patriarchy's paternal-god, known around the world variously as: Brahma, Zeus, Jupiter, Yahweh, Ra, Baal, Amma, Jesus, El, Odin, Osiris, Jehovah, Anu, Saturn, Bran, Adad, Enlil, Martu, Woden, and most commonly, God. The title "father" was frequently employed by biblical writers, who, in the Old Testament appended it to the Jewish version of the universal Father-God whom they called "Yahweh" (see for example, Psalms 89:26), while in the New Testament it was appended to the Christian version of the universal Father-God, known as "Jehovah"; see for example, Matthew 5:16; 1 Peter 1:2)

This, the matriarchal form, is used by Goddess-worshipers in place of the patriarchal version. Those goddesses who are called "Mother," or who are viewed as maternal figures, are many, of course. Among these are:

- Aka (Turkey)
- Ama (Semitic)
- Amba (India)
- Ba'Alat (Phoenicia)
- Bau (Babylon)
- Bontene (Greece)
- Ceres (Italy)
- Cybele (Phrygia)
- Cydippe (Greece)
- Damatres (Italy)
- Damkina (Akkadia)
- Deae Matres (Celtic)
- Demeter (Greece)
- Epona (Celtic Gaul)
- Eve (Semitic: Judeo-Christian)
- Frigga (Scandinavia)
- Genea (Phoenicia)
- Hera (Greece)
- Mami (Sumeria)
- Mary (Semitic: Judeo-Christian)
- Meter (Greece)
- Mut (Nubia/Egypt)
- Ocrisia (Italy)
- Oddudua (Nigeria)
- Ops (Italy)

▼ Pandora (Greece)
▼ Papa (Polynesia)
▼ Parvati (India)
▼ Renenet (Egypt)
▼ Selci Syt Emysyt (Siberia)
▼ Sundi-Mumi (Finland)
▼ Tellus Mater (Italy)
▼ Uti Hiata (North America: Pawnee)
▼ Utset (North America: Sia and Navaho)
▼ Vesta (Italy)
▼ Yemaya (Hispanic: Santeria)
▼ Zaramama (Peru)

To Westerners, no doubt, the best known Mother-Goddess is Christianity's Virgin Mary, a composite deity that slowly developed over many centuries, and who was lovingly portrayed on the cover of the first edition of this book.

While Mary herself was a historical person, biblically speaking the "Virgin Mary" began as a local Judaic form of the great Mediterranean and Near Eastern Pagan Mother-Goddess known far and wide as Ma, Mar, Mari, Maria, Mariam, Marian, Marie, Mer, or Meri.

To this figure various myths were gradually appended, along with the legends, titles and attributes of other Pagan Goddesses.

Among these are:

- ▼ Diana (the "God-Bearer")
- ▼ Ishtar (the Virgin Mother of the Savior Tammuz)
- ▼ Kore (the Virgin Mother of the Savior Aeon)
- ▼ Cybele (the Magna Mater, or "Great Mother" of the Gods)
- ▼ Aphrodite (the Love-Goddess after whom our month Aphrilis or "April" is named)
- ▼ Maia (the Virgin Mother of Hermes, and the Goddess after whom our month of "May" is named)
- ▼ Asherah (the Great Mother-Goddess worshiped by Solomon and other early Hebrew Goddess-worshipers; see 1 Kings 11:5)
- ▼ Nana (the Virgin Mother of the Savior Attis)
- ▼ Hecate (the Virgin Mother and "Queen of Heaven")
- ▼ Juno (the Virgin Mother of the Savior Mars, and the Goddess after whom our month of "June" is named)
- ▼ Isis (the Virgin Mother of the Savior Horus)
- ▼ Maya (the Virgin Mother of the Savior Buddha)
- ▼ The Moerae (the Greek all-female Holy Trinity)

During this Christianization process the shrines and temples of the Pagan goddesses were taken over by orthodox Christianity and converted into churches consecrated to Mary. In the 4th Century, for example, Diana's shrine at Ephesus was rededicated to Mary, while in Rome Magna Mater's sacred cave-shrine became the site on which the Cathedral of Santa Maria Maggiore was later built. At Philae the great temple of Isis was rededicated to Mary in the 6th Century, and on Cyprus Aphrodite's sanctuaries were transformed into "Mary's churches."

One of the more overt instances of assimilation in the creation of the Pagan-Christian Mother-Goddess, the Virgin Mary, came from the Hindu Mother-Goddess Aditi, whom devotees call the "Woman Clothed with the Sun." Aditi is portrayed in Indian sacred art wearing a crown of twelve stars (symbols of her twelve savior-sons, called the Adityas), riding on a crescent Moon (long one of the archetypal symbols of Goddess).

The Jewish-Christian mystics who penned the biblical book of Revelation adopted Aditi, and inserted her figure and image into the Twelfth Chapter as the "Mother of the New Jerusalem," known to contemporary Christians as the Virgin Mary (see Revelation 12:1). (See GODDESS; HEAVENLY MOTHER)

MOTHER, LADY OF HEAVEN AND EARTH (the patriarchal form is: "Father, Lord of heaven and earth," a phrase long used by the Patriarchy, and commonly employed by biblical writers; see for example, Matthew 11:25)

This, the matriarchal form, is used by Goddess-worshipers in place of the patriarchal version, as a title indicating Goddess' honor and esteem. (See GODDESS; MOTHER)

MOTHER WHICH IS IN HEAVEN, YOUR (the patriarchal form is: "your Father which is in heaven," a phrase long used by the Patriarchate, and commonly employed by biblical writers; see for example, Matthew 7:11)

This, the matriarchal form, is used by Goddess-worshipers in place of the patriarchal version, when addressing Goddess. (See

GODDESS; MOTHER; THE LADY'S PRAYER)

MOUNT OF GODDESS, THE (the patriarchal form is: "the mount of God," a phrase long used by the Patriarchy, and commonly employed by biblical writers; see for example, Exodus 24:13)

This, the matriarchal form, is used by Goddess-worshipers in place of the patriarchal version, in feminine sacred writings.

Actually, the ancient Jew's "Mount of God" had nothing to do with a male Father-God. Like all other ancient prepatriarchal religions, Judaism began as a polytheistic Goddess-worshiping faith, a matrifocal belief system that was built around Goddess' 364-day, thirteen-month Lunar Year, and the veneration of both her maternal beneficence and her parthenogenic reproductive power (see for example, Joshua 24:2, 14-15).

The names by which the ancient Jews' venerated Goddess were many: Shekhina, Wisdom, the Holy Spirit, the Community of Israel, the Word, Bath Qol, the Earth, the Mother City, Zion, and the Daughter of Zion. Even the Torah was named after her: Torah means "the Law," yet another early name for the Hebrew Goddess. She was most often called "Asherah" (or "Ashtoreth"), meaning the "Universal Law" of the Matriarch.

After the Patriarchal Takeover permeated Eurasia and the Near East (c. 1000 B.C. to 500 B.C.), however, Judaism—along with the matriarchal European religions—was patricized. In the process a male consort named "Yahweh" was imposed upon Asherah, creating a Divine Couple (or Androgyne), that was venerated for several centuries by Jews throughout the Near East.

Eventually, however, as the fallout from the Patriarchal Takeover gradually smothered nearly all vestiges of Goddess-worship, Asherah herself was finally ousted from the Hebrew Pantheon, leaving only her husband Yahweh to rule as the sole deity of Judaism (see for example, 2 Kings 5:15; Isaiah 45:5).

In the virulent anti-Goddess, anti-woman period that followed, Goddess' Temples were torn down (see for example, Acts 19:27), and her name was expunged from all sacred Jewish writings. In their place, patriarchal Jewish scribes and mythographers heaped scorn and ridicule on anything associated with the "Old Religion" of Goddess.

The entire second chapter of the book of Hosea, for instance, records God's fiery tirade against the "Great Harlot," that is, Asherah the Mother-Goddess (along with her followers' witch-like customs of holding sacred feasts at the new Moon), whom the "children of Israel" refused to cease from worshiping (see Hosea 2:1-23).

Indeed, in some ways the Old Testament seems to be little more than a detailed chronicle tracing the long and painful road of Near Eastern religion transforming itself from a gynocentric belief system to an androcentric one. Nearly every Old Testament book is rife with examples of the early Jews' many attempts to return to their old polytheistic Pagan ways (see for example, Joshua 23:7, 16; 24:23; Hosea 3:1; Judges 2:11-13, 17, 19; 3:5-7; 8:33-34; Ezekiel 8:14; Amos 5:26), their cherished orgiastic rituals (see for example, Judges 8:27; Jeremiah 3:6-9; Ezekiel 16:25-26; 23:37), and the worship of their beloved Goddess (see for example, 1 Kings 11:5, 31-33; 2 Kings 23:13). Two Jewish Queens, Maacha and Athaliah, are shown being dethroned or brutally murdered for attempting to revive Goddess-worship and reinstitute it back into Judaism (see 1 Kings 15; 2 Kings 11).

Despite the wholesale obliteration of Goddess from Reform, Conservative, and non-Hasidic Orthodox Judaism, traces of the female element can still be found among the Sephardim, the Oriental Jews, and the Hasidic Ashkenazim. The Old Testament itself retains numerous vestiges of a Judaism that began as a matriarchal religious culture focused around Goddess.

In passage after passage the biblical authors curiously describe their male god, Yahweh (or Jehovah or Jesus) in feminine terminology, functioning, not as a man, but as a woman. A careful reading of the Bible reveals that God is variously portrayed as a life-giving mother (Isaiah 42:14), a nursing mother (Isaiah 49:15), a midwife (Isaiah 66:9), a female pelican (Psalms 102:6), a mother bear (Hosea 13:8), a female homemaker (Psalms 123:1-2), a female lover (Song of Solomon 6:9), a bakerwoman (Luke 13:20-21), a mother eagle (Exodus 19:4), a mother hen (Matthew 23:27), and, copying the Pagan custom, as a Goddess of wisdom known as Hokhma (Proverbs 1:20-33).

In addition, Judaism retains its reliance on the thirteen-month Lunar Calender, once an integral aspect of the daily life of the early Goddess-worshiping Jews. Many other religions (such as Hinduism) and countries (for example, Saudi Arabia and Yemen) continue to rely on Goddess' Lunar Calender as well. Even

Christianity—which long ago adopted and Christianized all of Paganism's holy days—still calculates Easter (originally an ancient Goddess festival named after the Saxon Fertility-Goddess Eostre) on the Lunar Calender.

The symbol of Judaism, known as the Star of David or Solomon's Seal, is a remnant of Goddess-worship (borrowed by the Jews from Tantric Hinduism): the downward-pointing triangle of the Judaic hexagram (▽) is an archetypal symbol of the Female Principle; or more specifically, of Goddess' pubic triangle, the Holy Yoni out of which all life magically pours. The upward-pointing triangle of the Star of David (△) represents the Male Principle; or more literally, the erect lingam or phallus. When the two triangles are combined, the resulting hexagram (✡) symbolizes the spiritual-sexual union of the two genders, called by Kabbalists and other Jewish mystics, the "Great Yantra."

With Judaism's deep roots in Goddess-worship, it is not surprising that what the Bible calls "the Mount of God" actually turns out to be a feminine emblem, one honoring the Great Mother, not the Great Father.

The mountain has long been a Goddess archetype symbolizing her life-bearing pregnant abdomen, her nurturing milk-spewing breasts, and her swollen life-giving vulva. Indeed, the Hebrew word for mountain is *hara* (or *har* or *harar*) meaning "pregnant belly," while *hara* is in turn related to the Hebrew word *hora*, meaning a temple priestess who works under the auspices of Goddess, or what ancient Jews called a "whore."

The Hebrew word *hara* itself is a derivation of the Sanskrit word *Hariti*, which, thousands of years before the rise of Judaism, was the name of a great Indian Mountain-Mother-Goddess. One ancient Semitic tribe, the biblical Horites, claimed to be descended from the Whore-Goddess known as *Hora*, and so named themselves after her (see Genesis 36). The Persian Sun-God Ahura Mazda is still said to live in a brilliantly-lit palace on the summit of "Mount Hara," while the ancient Latins referred to those clairvoyant diviners who read the entrails of animals as *Haru-spices*, meaning "those who gaze into the belly."

Our modern words horoscope and hour both derive from the same feminine cognate: *hora*. Hence, there were the ancient *Horae*, or temple priestesses, who used to calculate the passage of time by performing magical circle dances. This method of time-keeping was necessary for the preparation of astrological charts which, as today, were based on precise hourly computations.

The modern science of measuring time is called "horology," while contemporary Judaism still retains a folk dance known as the "Hora." As I discuss in my book *Aphrodite's Trade*, both are named after the ancient sacred prostitutes, the *Horae* (religious "Whores") whose primary function was to teach men the Sexual Mysteries. The *Horae* were often seen symbolized in the great mammary-like mountains and vulva-like hills of the ancient world.

The myths, folk legends, and fairy tales of nearly all human societies and cultures contain countless references to "magic mountains," breast-like "twin peaks," and "Mother-mountains," that function as the maternal birthplace and home of various goddesses and gods.

Judeo-Christian mythology is no exception. However, the Bible's "Mount of God" is more correctly called the "Mount of Goddess," or as the Romans called a woman's vulva region, *Mons Veneris*; that is, the "Mount of (the Sex-Goddess) Venus," a deity later known to orthodox and mystical Christians as the Virgin Mother-Goddess, Mary. (See GODDESS ALMIGHTY)

A Christian woodcut showing the preaching of St. Bernardine of Siena (left), with Mary and the infant Jesus (right). Note Mary's crown of 12 stars, borrowed from the Pagan Goddess Aditi, and her lunar crescent platform, borrowed from the Pagan Goddess Astarte.

128 ∞ THE GODDESS DICTIONARY OF WORDS & PHRASES

"The Immaculate Conception," by Murillo, showing the Christian parthenogenic (virgin) Mother-Goddess Mary with the familiar Pagan female astro-symbol, the lunar crescent.

Sculpture of the Cyprian Aphrodite.

OH MY GODDESS! (the patriarchal form is: "Oh my God!")

This, the matriarchal form, is used by Goddess-worshipers in place of the patriarchal version, as an exclamatory phrase.

OUR MOTHER WHICH ART IN HEAVEN (the patriarchal form is: "Our Father which art in heaven," a phrase taken from the "Lord's Prayer" of the Judeo-Christian holy book, the Bible; see Matthew 6:9; Luke 11:2)

This, the matriarchal form, is used by Goddess-worshipers in place of the patriarchal version, when addressing the Supreme Being, Goddess. (See THE LADY'S PRAYER)

The Venus of Brassempouy.

Scandinavian Mother-Goddess Freya, Frigga, or Frig, after whom our weekday Friday is named.

PLAYING GODDESS (the patriarchal form is: "playing God")

    Indirectly, the phrase "playing God" implies that the male Father-God is the original creator of the Universe, and that in turn he governs the complex machinations of everyday life on Earth. This makes the term an oxymoron, for all of the earliest prepatriarchal myths maintain that it was Goddess, not God, who generated the Cosmos and all life in it.

    Indeed, the idea of a supreme male deity, or even a minor father-figure, did not emerge in human society until the Late Neolithic, the time of the Patriarchal Takeover (c. 4300 B.C.). After all, it is the human female, not the human male, that gives birth, an act still held to be parthenogenic by many living archaic peoples.

    Hence, this, the matriarchal form, is used by Goddess-worshipers in place of the patriarchal version, to denote the true Supreme "Creator": Goddess, the Great Mother and Creatrix. (See GODDESS; GODDESS CREATED THE HEAVEN AND THE EARTH; THE WORD OF GODDESS)

PRAISE GODDESS (the patriarchal form is: "Praise God")

    This, the matriarchal form, is used by Goddess-worshipers in place of the patriarchal version, as a salutation in honor of the

Supreme Being, Goddess.

PRAISE BE TO GODDESS (the patriarchal form is: "Praise be to God")

This, the matriarchal form, is used by Goddess-worshipers in place of the patriarchal version, as an ancient prayer-phrase that has long been used to honor the name of the Supreme Being, Goddess.

"The Diana of Ephesus" at the Vatican. Saint Paul attested to the global popularity of the universal Pagan Mother-Goddess (symbolized by the Roman Moon-Goddess Diana) when he bitterly complained that it was she, not God the Father, "whom all Asia and the world worshippeth" (Acts 19:27).

QUEENDOM OF GODDESS, THE (the patriarchal form is: "the kingdom of God," a phrase long used by the Patriarchy, and commonly employed by biblical writers; see for example, Matthew 6:33; Luke 18:29)

This, the matriarchal form, is used by Goddess-worshipers in place of the patriarchal version, to denote the realm governed by the Great Mother: Goddess.

QUEEN OF HEAVEN, THE (the patriarchal form is: "the King of Heaven," a phrase long used by the Patriarchy, and commonly employed by biblical writers; see for example, Daniel 4:37)

This, the matriarchal form, is used by Goddess-worshipers in place of the patriarchal version, as one of Goddess' more popular titles. (For ancient biblical references to Goddess under this title, see for example, Jeremiah 7:18; 44:19. Also, Jesus is shown referring to Goddess in her Egyptian form as "the Queen of the South," a reference to the great Moon-Goddess, known across the ancient Near East as the "Queen of Sheba"—that is, the "Queen of Seven," one of Goddess' holiest numbers; see for example, Matthew 12:42; Luke 11:31.)

QUEEN OF QUEENS (the patriarchal form is: "King of kings," a phrase long used by the Patriarchy, and commonly employed by biblical writers; see for example, Ezra 7:11; Ezekiel 26:7; Daniel 2:37. It is also applied by Christians to the Christian Father-God Jehovah in his Son-God form, "Jesus"; see for example, 1 Timothy 6:15; Revelation 17:14; 19:16)

This, the matriarchal form, is used by Goddess-worshipers in place of the patriarchal version, as one of Goddess' many titles of omnipotence. (See GODDESS; MOTHER; HEAVENLY MOTHER: QUEEN OF HEAVEN, THE)

Astarte in Cyprus.

RENDER UNTO CAESAR THE THINGS THAT ARE CAESAR'S, AND UNTO GODDESS THE THINGS THAT ARE GODDESS' (the patriarchal form is: "Render unto Caesar the things that are Caesar's, and unto God the things that are God's," an expression taken from the Christian holy book of Matthew; see 22:21)

This, the matriarchal form, is used by Goddess-worshipers in place of the patriarchal version.

This maxim—which holds that though we are spirits temporarily encased in physical bodies, while here on Earth we must be careful to obey Earthly laws—is not original to Christianity. It is found in the teachings and writings of numerous pre-Christian Pagan mystics and religious leaders.

Venus and Anchises.

Venus with shield and pencil.

S

SHE (JUNO, that is GODDESS) HAS FAVORED OUR UNDERTAKING (the patriarchal form is: "He (Jupiter, that is God) has favored our undertaking," a saying taken from Virgil's *Aeneid*)

This, the matriarchal form, is used by Goddess-worshipers in place of the patriarchal version. Its Latin form, *Annuit Coeptis* (from *anno*, "to favor," and *coeptis*, "endeavors"), appears on the reverse side of the great seal of the U.S.A., found on the back side of the one-dollar bill.

While the saying *Annuit Coeptis* has long been considered a patriarchal masculine saying, this is only a modern coverup. For like most of the other words (and symbols) on the one-dollar bill, this too is deeply and occultly connected to Goddess-worship.

Annuit is a play on the names of two ancient Goddesses: Anna and Nuit (also known as Nut). The mystical numerological value of the word *annuit*, namely 390, is the same as the phrase "Mother of God," while the word *coeptis* shares the same Masonic value as the name of the Goddess Aphrodite: 317. The phrase *Annuit Coeptis* itself is identical in cabalistic value to the Virgin Mary (that is, 707), another one of tens of thousands of embodiments of the universal "Mother of God." (See GODDESS HAS SMILED ON OUR ACCOMPLISHMENTS; IN GODDESS WE TRUST)

SHE (GODDESS) WHO TRANSPLANTED SUSTAINS (the patriarchal form is: "He (God) who transplanted sustains," the motto of Connecticut)

This, the matriarchal form, is used by Goddess-worshipers in place of the patriarchal version, in Connecticut and elsewhere.

SO HELP YOU GODDESS (the patriarchal form is: "so help you God," a phrase that derives from the American court system, which requires of its witnesses the following pledge: "Do you promise to tell the whole truth, and nothing but the truth, so help you God?" Many courts now no longer require the last four words since 1) they violate the Jeffersonian idea of separation of church and state; 2) they offend nonbelievers; and 3) they are an affront to Goddess-worshipers; your author, however, believes that this phrase, as it is used in U.S. courts, should not have been tampered with)

This, the matriarchal form, is used by Goddess-worshipers in place of the patriarchal version, to imbue a pledge with an individual's faith and belief in Goddess. (See SWEAR TO GODDESS)

SPIRIT OF GODDESS, THE (the patriarchal form is: "the spirit of God," a phrase long used by the Patriarchy, and commonly employed by biblical writers; see for example, Exodus 31:3)

This, the matriarchal form, is used by Goddess-worshipers in place of the patriarchal version, to denote the essence of the Female Principle.

The idea of "the spirit of God" is incongruous; it is, in fact, an oxymoron. For, according to all prepatriarchal religious traditions, the Spirit, or rather spirit, is feminine, not masculine.

Evidence of this can be found in the Christian entity known as "the Holy Spirit," or "the Holy Ghost," which first appears in prehistoric religions as a Pagan Virgin-Goddess who formed the Universe using her divine breath (insufflation). One of her sacred animals is the dove, an archetypal emblem of feminine peacefulness and gentleness.

The Virgin-Goddess is but one of three female deities who comprises the original Holy Trinity, known throughout the Pagan religions as the Triple-Goddess. Here, the Virgin symbolizes the birth of life; the second Goddess, the Mother, symbolizes the nurturing of life; and the third Goddess, the Grandmother (or Crone), symbolizes the termination of life.

In seeking models on which to build a Christian version of the Pagan Trinity, the early Church Fathers assimilated the Triple-Goddess and masculinized her, transforming this archetypal feminine triadic deity into "the Father, the Son, and the Holy Ghost." In this way, the Virgin-Creatress became the "Holy Spirit," and her sacred animal, the dove, was appended to the baptism story of Jesus (Luke 3:22).

To this day, the Christian Church continues to be ambiguous about the true nature and origins of the Holy Spirit, calling it a "genderless entity." (See CRONE, MOTHER, AND VIRGIN-DAUGHTER; GODDESS BLESS YOU; WORD OF GODDESS, THE)

SWEAR TO GODDESS (the patriarchal form is: "swear to God")

This, the matriarchal form, is used by Goddess-worshipers in place of the patriarchal version, as an oath-taking pledge performed under the auspices of Goddess. (See SO HELP YOU GODDESS)

Aphrodite of Alcamenes, known in ancient Rome as Venus Genetrix.

THANK GODDESS! (the patriarchal form is: "Thank God!")

    This, the matriarchal form, is used by Goddess-worshipers in place of the patriarchal version, as an ancient benediction meant to show gratitude to the Supreme Being, Goddess.

THANKS BE TO GODDESS (the patriarchal form is: "Thanks be to God")

    This, the matriarchal form, is used by Goddess-worshipers in place of the patriarchal version, most particularly when an enterprise comes to a successful conclusion.

TO GODDESS, THE BEST, THE GREATEST (the patriarchal form is: "To God, the best, the greatest")

    This, the matriarchal form, is used by Goddess-worshipers in place of the patriarchal version.

    In ancient times the masculine Latin form of this phrase, *Deo optimo maximo*, was abbreviated as "D.O.M.," and used as a dedication on works of art and in books. Here we have substituted *Dea* ("Goddess") for *Deo* ("God"), so it now reads: *Dea optimo maximo*. Hence, the abbreviation D.O.M. continues to appear as a dedication to Goddess in art and literature.

TO THE GREATER GLORY OF GODDESS (the patriarchal form is: "to the greater glory of God," the motto of the Society of Jesus)

This, the matriarchal form, is used by Goddess-worshipers in place of the patriarchal version, as a toast or salutation for religious purposes, or for sacred or secular feasts honoring the Great Mother: Goddess.

TO THE LADY GODDESS, SUPREME RULER OF THE WORLD (the patriarchal form is: "To the Lord God, supreme ruler of the world," the motto of the Benedictine Order)

This, the matriarchal form, is used by Goddess-worshipers in place of the patriarchal version, as a toast or salutation for religious purposes, or for sacred or secular feasts honoring the Great Mother: Goddess.

The Venus head, Museum of Bardos.

U

UNDER GODDESS (the patriarchal form is: "under God")

For both feminists and Goddess-worshipers living in the U.S.A., the Pledge of Allegiance has long been a source of friction and controversy. As pertains to the linguistic focus of this dictionary, there has been one primary reason: the pledge's use of the phrase, "under God." Interestingly, in the original pledge, composed by the American socialist Francis Bellamy (also a member of the United States Flag Association) in 1892, the phrase "under God" is entirely absent.

Indeed, in Bellamy's version, there is no mention of "God" at all. In fact, the phrase did not appear in the Pledge of Allegiance until sixty-two years later, when it was purposefully introduced by the U.S. Congress in 1954. (America's traditional Southerners, like myself, also have reservations with our controversial Pledge. For more on this particular topic, see my book *Abraham Lincoln: The Southern View*.)

Since a majority of Americans have chosen to violate the First Amendment by partially tearing down the wall that separates Church and State, why not allow the nation's citizens to choose the deity they wish to pledge under? For many the choice would be obvious: they would select Goddess, not God. For the latter did not appear on the religious scene until a mere 6,000 years ago, while the former was the only Supreme Being revered by humanity from at least 500,000 B.C. to 4300 B.C. We are speaking here of none other than the female deity known around the world as the "Divine Mother and Creatress of All Life."

The new Goddess Pledge of Allegiance reads as follows:

> "I pledge allegiance to the flag of the United States of America, and to the Republic for which it stands, one nation under Goddess, indivisible, with liberty and justice for all."

This, the matriarchal form, is now used by Goddess-worshipers in place of the patriarchal version.

UNGODDESSLY (the patriarchal form is: "ungodly")

This, the matriarchal form, is used by Goddess-worshipers as an adjective in place of the patriarchal version. It refers to either the denial of Goddess, or to the state or quality of being disobedient, impious, outrageous, or irreligious. (See GODDESSLY)

UNGODDESSLINESS (the patriarchal form is: "ungodliness")

This, the matriarchal form, is used by Goddess-worshipers as a noun in place of the patriarchal version, to refer to the state or quality of being ungoddessly. (See GODDESSLY; UNGODDESSLY)

VOICE OF THE PEOPLE IS THE VOICE OF GODDESS, THE

(the patriarchal form is: "The voice of the people is the voice of God")

    This, the matriarchal form, is used by Goddess-worshipers in place of the patriarchal version, as a political feminine anthem.

Relief of the Birth of Goddess, in this case, Venus.

"Adam and Eve in Paradise," by Doré. Both Adam and Eve, the Semitic "first man and woman," were motifs borrowed by the writers of the Old Testament from the creation legends of far earlier societies.

Ancient goddess with pedestal.

WITH GODDESS' FAVOR (the patriarchal form is: "With God's Favor")

    This, the matriarchal form, is used by Goddess-worshipers in place of the patriarchal version, as an ancient phrase to invoke the aid of the Supreme Being, Goddess.

WITH GODDESS' HELP (the patriarchal form: "With God's Help")

    This, the matriarchal form, is used by Goddess-worshipers in place of the patriarchal version, as an ancient expression to invoke the help of the Supreme Being, Goddess.

WHOM GODDESS WISHES TO DESTROY, SHE FIRST MAKES MAD (the patriarchal form is: "Whom God wishes to destroy, he first makes mad," a rendering from a line by Euripides)

    This, the matriarchal form, is used by Goddess-worshipers in place of the patriarchal version.

WOMAN OF GODDESS (the patriarchal form is: "man of God," a phrase long used by the Patriarchy, and commonly employed by biblical writers; see for example, Joshua 14:6; Judges 13:6; Nehemiah 12:24; 1 Timothy 6:11)

This, the matriarchal form, is used by Goddess-worshipers in place of the patriarchal version. In prepatriarchal times (that is, before 4300 B.C.), all women *and* men were seen as "children (or daughters and sons) of Goddess."

More specifically, the designation "woman of Goddess" once indicated a female spiritual guide, temple priestess, sacred prostitute, or holy healer, who worked under the authority of Goddess.

Today, organized mainstream religions may use the term for female ministers, while in mystical and gynocentric religions it can now apply to priestesses, or simply female members. In general, however, the term "woman of Goddess" covers all women. (See CHILD OF GODDESS; CHILDREN OF GODDESS)

WOMAN PROPOSES, GODDESS DISPOSES (the patriarchal form is: "Man proposes, God disposes," a quote taken from Virgil's *Aeneid*)

This, the matriarchal form, is used by Goddess-worshipers in place of the patriarchal version, as a motto that justifies an unsuccessful endeavor, or to portray the frailties of humanity in comparison with the omnipotent powers of the Supreme Being: Goddess.

WOMAN UPSTAIRS, THE (the patriarchal form is: "the Man upstairs")

This, the matriarchal form, is used by Goddess-worshipers in place of the patriarchal version, in reference to the Supreme

Being: Goddess.

WORD OF GODDESS, THE (the patriarchal form is: "the Word of God," a phrase long used by the Patriarchy, and commonly employed by biblical writers; see for example, 1 Samuel 9:27)

This, the matriarchal form, is used in place of the patriarchal version. The Bible states that "in the beginning was the Word, and the Word was with God, and the Word was God" (John 1:1).

However, the historical truth is that it was Goddess, the Great Mother, who first invented not only the alphabet, language, and writing, but the Divine Logos as well. Indeed, prepatriarchal, pre-biblical creation myths tell how Goddess used word-power, or her sacred breath, to create life (insufflation).

In pre-Christian Egypt, for instance, it was the Goddess Maat whose "Word is Truth"; in pre-Christian Greece it was the Goddess Hecate who created the "Word Made Flesh"; while in pre-Christian India it was the Goddess Kali (in Ireland known as Kelle) who held the "Holy Word of Creation."

As paternity was unknown in the ancient world, women who bore children were thought to be parthenogenic, or self-fertilizing virgins, who generated life within themselves by breathing on, or by performing a mantra over, their pregnant bellies. (Men could thus only procure legal, political, familial, or economic power, through sexual intercourse with a woman, a "daughter of Goddess," the sole possessor of the procreative Logos.)

In this way the Indian Goddess Vac was said to have engendered the material world through the sacred sound "Om" (a word meaning "pregnant belly"), the Primordial Logos known as "the supreme syllable, the mother of all sound." (Our modern word "navel" derives from the Old High German word *nabalo*, which is in turn related to the Greek word *om-phalos*, meaning "navel," or "the center.")

It was thus that for thousands of years, prehistoric women practiced the custom of imbuing their newborn infants with souls by blowing into their mouths or on them, or by naming them as they nursed at the breast (matronymicism or metronymy).

The parthenogenic Mother-Goddess who spontaneously generates life is a common motif, one found in the religions and myths of nearly every culture and society, including the West and Christianity. Among the great Virgin-Mothers of the world we have:

▼ Aditi (India)
▼ Arianrhod (Wales)
▼ Asase Yaa (Africa: Ashanti)
▼ Ataensic (North America: Iroquois)
▼ Bugan (Philippines)
▼ Ceto (Greece)
▼ Dechtere (Ireland)
▼ Diti (India)
▼ Djanggawul Sisters (Australia)
▼ Djigonasee (North America: Seneca, Cayuga, Onondaga,

Oneida, Mohawk, Tuscarora)
▼ Eurynome (Greece)
▼ Finchoem (Ireland)
▼ Fu-Pao (China)
▼ Gaea (Greece)
▼ Henwen (England)
▼ Hera (Greece)
▼ Kongsim (Korea)
▼ Ligoapup (Micronesia)
▼ Luminu-Ut (Oceania: Minahassa)
▼ Mary (Semitic: Judeo-Christian)
▼ Mu Olokukurtilisop (Panama: Cuna)
▼ Nana (Phrygia)
▼ Neith (Egypt)
▼ Nessa (Ireland)
▼ Nyx (Greece)
▼ Parvati (India)
▼ Poza-Mama (Siberia)
▼ Shiwanokia (North America: Zuni)
▼ Tai Yuan (China)
▼ Thalassa (Greece)
▼ Tiamat (Babylonia)
▼ Wari-Ma-Te-Takere (Polynesia)
▼ Wawalag Sisters (Australia)

After the Patriarchal Takeover (c. 4300 B.C.), the two themes of parthenogenesis and procreation-by-way-of-magic words, were adopted by male-dominant societies, who began to develop myths in which male gods created life through the power of their sacred utterances and holy breath. (In the process, women lost the right of mother-naming—that is, the right to name their children—as men began naming their offspring after themselves.) Thus, an early pre-Christian savior-christ, the Phrygian Sun-God and Savior, Attis, for instance, was hailed across the ancient world as "the Logos who holds the universe together."

About this same time, the Jewish Father-God Yahweh (known formerly to the Greeks as Zeus, to the Romans as Jupiter, and subsequently to Christians as Jehovah), was also given the power of Goddess' Divine Logos (see for example, Ezekiel 37:5). To this day Judeo-Christian mythology holds that God created humanity by breathing life into a lump of clay (Genesis 2:7).

Later, Christianity would hold that its own Sun-God (or Son-God), Jesus, was also an incarnation of "the Word of Goddess Made Flesh," the Divine Logos (John 1:14). Under the new Patriarchy, however, Jesus was given the androcentric title, "the Word of God" (Revelation 19:13). Adding to this biblical confusion, Jesus was also imbued with the strictly female ability of insufflation, one of the Pagan Mother-Goddess' many astounding procreative powers (John 20:22). (See GODDESS; GODDESS BLESS YOU; GODDESS CREATED THE HEAVEN AND THE EARTH)

WORD OF THE LADY, THE (the patriarchal form is: "the word of the Lord," a phrase long used by the Patriarchate, and commonly employed by biblical writers; see for example, Genesis 15:1)

This, the matriarchal form, is used by Goddess-worshipers in place of the patriarchal version, when referring to the tenets of the Great Mother: Goddess (See THE WORD OF GODDESS)

WRATH OF GODDESS, THE (the patriarchal form is: "the wrath God," a phrase long used by the Patriarchate, and commonly employed by biblical writers; see for example, Psalms 78:31; John 3:36; Revelation 14:10)

This, the matriarchal form, is used by Goddess-worshipers in place of the patriarchal version, when referring to Goddess' anger and indignation at the behavior of her earthly children.

The End

Carrying in procession the symbol of Istar or Ishtar.

BIBLIOGRAPHY

And Suggested Reading

Adler, Margot. *Drawing Down the Moon*. Boston, MA: Beacon Press, 1981.

Agha-Jaffar, Tamara. *Women and Goddesses in Myth and Sacred Text*. New York, NY: Longman, 2004.

Albright, William Powell. *Yahweh and the Gods of Canaan*. New York, NY: Doubleday, 1968.

Allen, Paula Gunn. *The Sacred Hoop: Recovering the Feminine in American Indian Traditions*. Boston, MA: Beacon Press, 1986.

Allison, Dale C., Jr. *Resurrecting Jesus: The Earliest Christian Tradition and Its Interpreters*. New York, NY: T and T Clark, 2005.

Andrews, Ted. *The Occult Christ: Angelic Mysteries, Seasonal Rituals, and the Divine Feminine*. St. Paul, MN: Llewellyn, 1993.

Angus, Samuel. *The Mystery-Religions and Christianity: A Study of the Religious Background of Early Christianity*. 1925. New York, NY: Citadel Press, 1966 ed.

Ardrey, Robert. *African Genesis*. 1961. New York, NY: Dell, 1972 ed.

——. *The Territorial Imperative*. 1966. New York, NY: Delta, 1968 ed.

Armstrong, Herbert W., Keith W. Stump, and John Halford. *The Plain Truth About Christmas*. 1952. Pasadena, CA: Worldwide Church of God, 1986 ed.

Armstrong, Karen. *A History of God: The 4000-Year Quest of Judaism, Christianity and Islam*. New York, NY: Knopf, 1993.

Ashe, Geoffrey. *The Virgin: Mary's Cult and the Re-emergence of the Goddess*. 1976. London, UK: Arkana, 1988 ed.

——. *Dawn Behind the Dawn: A Search for the Earthly Paradise*. New York, NY: Henry Holt, 1992.

Atkins, Gaius Glenn, and Charles Samuel Braden. *Procession of the Gods*. 1930. New York, NY: Harper and Brothers Publishers, 1936 ed.

Attwater, Donald. *The Penguin Dictionary of Saints.* 1965. Harmondsworth, UK: Penguin, 1983 ed.

Avalon, Arthur. *Shakti and Shakta.* New York, NY: Dover, 1978.

Ayto, John. *Dictionary of Word Origins.* New York, NY: Arcade, 1990.

Bachofen, Johann Jakob. *Myth, Religion and Mother Right.* Princeton, NJ: Princeton University Press, 1967.

Baigent, Michael. *The Jesus Papers: Exposing the Greatest Cover-Up in History.* San Francisco, CA: Harper San Francisco, 2006.

Baigent, Michael, and Richard Leigh. *The Dead Sea Scrolls Deception.* 1991. New York, NY: Touchstone, 1993 ed.

Baigent, Michael, Richard Leigh, and Henry Lincoln. *Holy Blood, Holy Grail.* 1982. New York, NY: Dell, 1983. ed.

———. *The Messianic Legacy.* New York, NY: Dell, 1986.

Baring, Anne, and Jules Cashford. *The Myth of the Goddess: Evolution of an Image.* 1991. Harmondsworth, UK: Arkana, 1993 ed.

Baring-Gould, Sabine. *Curious Myths of the Middle Ages.* New York, NY: University Books, 1967.

Barnstone, Willis (ed.). *The Other Bible: Ancient Esoteric Texts.* New York, NY: Harper and Row, 1984.

Baroja, Julio Caro. *The World of Witches.* Chicago, IL: University of Chicago Press, 1965.

Barraclough, Geoffrey, and Norman Stone (eds.). *The Times Atlas of World History.* 1978. Maplewood, NJ: Hammond, 1989 ed.

Baumgartner, Anne S. *A Comprehensive Dictionary of the Gods: From Abaasy to Zvoruna.* New York, NY: University Books, 1984.

Bauvel, Robert, and Adrian Gilbert. *The Orion Mystery: Unlocking the Secrets of the Pyramids.* New York, NY: Three Rivers Press, 1995.

Bayley, Harold. *Archaic England: An Essay in Deciphering Prehistory From Megalithic Monuments, Earthworks, Customs, Coins, Place-names, and Faerie Superstitions.* London, UK: Chapman and Hall, 1920.

Beard, Henry, and Christopher Cerf. *The Official Politically Correct Dictionary and Handbook.* New York, NY: Villard Books, 1993.

Bede. *Historia Ecclesiastica Gentis Anglorum* (*A History of the English Church and People*, Leo Sherley-Price, trans.). C.E. 731. Harmondsworth, UK: Penguin, 1955 (1974 ed.).

Begg, Ean. *The Cult of the Black Virgin*. Harmondsworth, UK: Arkana, 1985.

Bell, Robert E. *Women of Classical Mythology: A Biographical Dictionary*. 1991. Oxford, UK: Oxford University Press, 1993 ed.

Besant, Annie. *Esoteric Christianity or the Lesser Mysteries*. London, UK: Theosophical Publishing Society, 1905.

Best, Robert M. *Noah's Ark and the Ziusudra Epic: Sumerian Origins of the Flood Myth*. Fort Myers, FL: Enlil Press, 1999.

Bhagavad Gita (Juan Mascaró, trans.). c. 500 BC. Harmondsworth, UK: Penguin, 1962.

Biedermann, Hans. *Dictionary of Symbolism: Cultural Icons and the Meanings Behind Them* (James Hulbert, trans.). 1989. New York, NY: Facts On File, 1992 ed.

Bierlein, John Francis. *Parallel Myths*. New York, NY: Ballantine Wellspring, 1994.

Binder, Pearl. *Magic Symbols of the World*. London, UK: Hamlyn, 1972.

Boardman, John, Jasper Griffin, and Oswyn Murray (eds.). *The Roman World*. 1986. Oxford, UK: Oxford University Press, 1988 ed.

Boates, Karen Scott (ed.). *The Goddess Within*. Philadelphia, PA: Running Press, 1990.

Bostwick, Arthur Elmore (ed.). *Doubleday's Encyclopedia*. 1931. New York, NY: Doubleday, Doran, and Co., 1939 ed.

Bouquet, Alan Coates. *Comparative Religion: A Survey and Comparison of the Great Religions of the World*. London, UK: Penguin, 1942.

Bowden, John. *Archaeology and the Bible*. Austin, TX: American Atheist Press, 1982.

Branston, Brian. *Gods of the North*. London, UK: Thames and Hudson, 1955.

Bratton, Fred Gladstone. *Myths and Legends of the Ancient Near East: Great*

Stories of the Sumero-Akkadian, Egyptian, Ugaritic-Canaanite, and Hittite Cultures. New York, NY: Thomas Y. Crowell, 1970.

Breasted, James Henry. *Ancient Records of Egypt.* 5 vols. Chicago: IL: University of Chicago Press, 1906.

Brewster, Harold Pomeroy. *Saints and Festivals of the Christian Church.* New York, NY: Frederick A. Stokes, 1904.

Bridgwater, William (ed.). *The Columbia-Viking Desk Encyclopedia.* 1953. New York, NY: Viking Press, 1968 ed.

Briffault, Robert Stephen. *The Mothers: The Matriarchal Theory of Social Origins.* 1927. New York, NY: Macmillan, 1931 (single volume, abridged) ed.

Briggs, Katherine. *The Vanishing People: Fairy Lore and Legends.* New York, NY: Pantheon, 1978.

Brownrigg, Ronald. *Who's Who in the New Testament.* 1971. New York, NY: Oxford University Press, 1993 ed.

Bucke, Richard Maurice. *Cosmic Consciousness: A Study in the Evolution of the Human Mind.* 1901. New York, NY: Dutton, 1969 ed.

Budapest, Zsuzsanna Emese. *The Holy Book of Women's Mysteries* (Part 1). 1979. Oakland, CA: Susan B. Anthony Coven No. 1, 1982 ed.

——. *The Holy Book of Women's Mysteries* (Part 2). 1980. Oakland, CA: Susan B. Anthony Coven No. 1, 1982 ed.

Budge, Ernest Alfred Wallis. *Egyptian Magic.* London, UK: Kegan, Paul, Trench, Trübner, and Co., 1901.

——. *Osiris and the Egyptian Resurrection.* Vol. 1. London, UK: Philip Lee Warner, 1911.

——. *Amulets and Talismans.* 1930. New York, NY: Citadel, 1992 ed.

Bulfinch, Thomas. *Bulfinch's Mythology: The Age of Fable, the Age of Chivalry, Legends of Charlemagne.* New York, NY: Thomas Y. Crowell, 1913.

Bullough, Vern L., and Bonnie Bullough. *The Subordinate Sex: A History of Attitudes Toward Women.* 1973. Baltimore, MD: Penguin, 1974 ed.

Burn, A. R. *The Pelican History of Greece*. 1965. Harmondsworth, UK: Penguin, 1968 ed.

Burne, Jerome (ed.). *Chronicle of the World*. Mount Kisco, NY: Ecam Publications, 1989.

Butler, Trent C. (gen. ed.). *Holman Bible Dictionary*. Nashville, TN: Holman Bible Publishers, 1991.

Caesar, Gaius Julius. *The Conquest of Gaul [Gallic War]* (S. A. Handford, trans.). 51 B.C.E. Harmondsworth, UK: Penguin, 1951, 1988 ed.

Calvocoressi, Peter. *Who's Who in the Bible*. 1987. Harmondsworth, UK: Penguin, 1990 ed.

Campanelli, Pauline. *Ancient Ways: Reclaiming Pagan Traditions*. 1991. St. Paul, MN: 1992 ed.

Campbell, Joseph. *The Masks of God: Primitive Mythology*. Vol. 1. 1959. Harmondsworth, UK: Arkana, 1991 ed.

———. *The Masks of God: Oriental Mythology*. Vol. 2. 1962. Harmondsworth, UK: Arkana, 1991 ed.

———. *The Masks of God: Occidental Mythology*. Vol. 3. 1964. Harmondsworth, UK: Arkana, 1991 ed.

———. *The Masks of God: Creative Mythology*. Vol. 4. 1968. Harmondsworth, UK: Arkana, 1991 ed.

———. *Myths to Live By*. New York, NY: Bantam, 1972.

———. *The Power of Myth* (with Bill Moyers). New York, NY: Doubleday, 1988.

———. *Transformations of Myth Through Time*. New York, NY: Harper and Row, 1990.

Camphausen, Rufus C. *The Encyclopedia of Erotic Wisdom*. Rochester, VT: Inner Traditions International, 1991.

Capek, Mary Ellen S. (ed.). *A Woman's Thesaurus: An Index of Language Used to Describe and Locate Information By and About Women*. New York, NY: HarperCollins, 1989.

Carlyon, Richard. *A Guide to the Gods: An Essential Guide to World Mythology*.

New York, NY: Quill, 1981.

Carpenter, Edward. *Pagan and Christian Creeds: Their Origin and Meaning*: New York, NY: Blue Ribbon, 1920.

Carson, Anne. *Goddesses and Wise Women: The Literature of Feminist Spirituality, An Annotated Bibliography (1980-1992)*. Freedom, CA: Crossing Press, 1992.

Carter, Jesse Benedict. *The Religious Life of Ancient Rome: A Study in the Development of Religious Consciousness, From the Foundation of the City Until the Death of Gregory the Great*. Boston, MA: Houghton Mifflin, 1911.

Carus, Paul. *The Venus of Milo: An Archaeological Study of the Goddess of Womanhood*. London, UK: Open Court Publishing Co., 1916.

Cassius, Dio. *The Roman History: The Reign of Augustus* (Ian Scott-Kilvert, trans.). C. 214-226. Harmondsworth, UK: Penguin, 1988.

Cavendish, Richard. *A History of Magic*. 1987. Harmondsworth, UK: Arkana, 1990 ed.

Chetwynd, Tom. *Dictionary of Sacred Myth* ("Language of the Unconscious," Vol. 3). London, UK: Aquarian Press, 1986.

Christie-Murray, David. *A History of Heresy*. Oxford, UK: Oxford University Press, 1976.

Cirlot, J. E. *A Dictionary of Symbols*. 1962. New York, NY: Philosophical Library, 1983 ed.

Collins, Sheila D. *A Different Heaven and Earth: A Feminist Perspective on Religion*. Valley Forge, PA: Judson Press, 1974.

Comay, Joan. *Who's Who in the Old Testament (Together with the Apocrypha)*. 1971. New York, NY: Oxford University Press, 1993 ed.

Condon, R. J. *Our Pagan Christmas*. Austin, TX: American Atheist Press, 1989.

Constable, George (ed.). *Mysteries of the Unknown: Mystic Places*. Richmond, VA: Time-Life Books, Inc., 1987.

Cotterell, Arthur. *A Dictionary of World Mythology*. 1979. New York, NY: Oxford University Press, 1990 ed.

———. *The Macmillan Illustrated Encyclopedia of Myths and Legends*. New York, NY: Macmillan, 1989.

Cross, Frank L., and Elizabeth A. Livingstone. *The Oxford Dictionary of the Christian Church*. 1957. London, UK: Oxford University Press, 1974 ed.

Crossley-Holland, Kevin. *The Norse Myths*. New York, NY: Pantheon, 1980.

Cumont, Franz Valéry Marie. *The Mysteries of Mithra*. New York, NY: Dover, 1956.

———. *Oriental Religions in Roman Paganism*. New York, NY: Dover, 1956.

———. *Astrology and Religion Among the Greeks and Romans*. New York, NY: Dover, 1960.

Curtis, Vesta Sarkhosh. *Persian Myths: The Legendary Past*. Austin, TX: University of Texas Press, 1993.

Dalley, Stephanie (trans.). *Myths From Mesopotamia: Creation, the Flood, Gilgamesh, and Others*. 1989. Oxford, UK: Oxford University Press, 2008 ed.

Daly, Mary. *Beyond God the Father: Toward a Philosophy of Women's Liberation*. Boston, MA: Beacon Press, 1973.

Darlison, Bill. *The Gospel and the Zodiac: The Secret Truth About Jesus*. New York, NY: Overlook Press, 2008.

Davidson, Gustav. *A Dictionary of Angels*. 1967. New York, NY: The Free Press, 1971 ed.

Davidson, Hilda Roderick Ellis. *Gods and Myths of Northern Europe*. 1964. London, UK: Penguin, 1990 ed.

Davis, Frederick Hadland. *Myths and Legends of Japan*. 1913. Mineola, NY: Dover, 1992 ed.

———. *Pagan Scandinavia*. New York, NY: Frederick A. Praeger, 1967.

———. *Gods and Myths of the Viking Age*. New York, NY: Bell, 1981.

———. *Myths and Symbols in Pagan Europe: Early Scandinavian and Celtic Religions*. Syracuse, NY: Syracuse University Press, 1988.

Davis, John J. *Biblical Numerology: A Basic Study of the Use of Numbers in the*

Bible. 1968. Grand Rapids, MI: Baker Book House, 1988 ed.

Decker, Ed, and Dave Hunt. *The God Makers: A Shocking Expose of What the Mormon Church Really Believes*. Eugene, OR: Harvest House, 1984.

Delaney, John J. *Pocket Dictionary of Saints*. 1980. New York, NY: Image, 1983 (abridged) ed.

Delehaye, Hippolyte. *The Legends of the Saints: An Introduction to Hagiography*. New York, NY: Fordham University Press, 1962.

Dennis, Rabbi Geoffrey W. *The Encyclopedia of Jewish Myth, Magic and Mysticism*. Woodbury, MN: Llewellyn, 2007.

Derk, Francis H. *A Pocket Guide to the Names of Christ*. 1969. Minneapolis, MN: Bethany House, 1976 ed.

De Rosa, Peter. *Vicars of Christ: The Dark Side of the Papacy*. New York, NY: Crown Publishers, 1988.

de Volney, Constantin François. *The Ruins, or, A Survey of the Revolutions of Empires*. 1791. London, UK: James Watson, 1857 ed.

de Voragine, Jacobus. *The Golden Legend, or Lives of the Saints*. 7 vols. C. 1260. London, UK: J. M. Dent and Co., 1900.

Didron, M. *Christian Iconography; or, The History of Christian Art in the Middle Ages*. 2 vols. London, UK: Henry G. Bohn, 1851.

Dione, R. L. *Is God Supernatural?: The 4,000-Year Misunderstanding*. New York, NY: Bantam, 1976.

Doane, Thomas William. *Bible Myths and Their Parallels in Other Religions*. New York, NY: University Books, 1971.

Dorward, David. *Scottish Surnames: A Guide to the Family Names of Scotland*. Glasgow, Scotland: Harper Collins, 1995.

Dowley, Tim (ed.). *The History of Christianity*. 1977. Oxford, UK: Lion Publishing, 1990 ed.

Downing, Christine. *The Goddess: Mythological Images of the Feminine*. New York, NY: Crossroads Publishing, 1984.

Dumond, Val. *The Elements of Nonsexist Usage: A Guide to Inclusive Spoken and Written English*. Upper Saddle River, NJ: Prentice Hall, 1990.

Durant, Will. *The Story of Civilization: Volume 1—Our Oriental Heritage*.

1935. New York, NY: Simon and Schuster, 1954 ed.

Eban, Abba. *Heritage: Civilization and the Jews*. New York, NY: Summit, 1984.

Egyptian Book of the Dead, The (E. A. Wallis Budge, trans.). 1895. New York, NY: Dover, 1967 ed.

Ehrlich, Eugene. *Amo, Amas, Amat, and More*. New York, NY: Perennial Library, 1985.

Eisler, Riane. *The Chalice and the Blade: Our History, Our Future*. New York, NY: Perennial, 1987.

Elder, Dorothy. *From Metaphysical to Mystical: A Study of the Way*. Denver, CO: Doriel Publishing Co., 1992.

Eliade, Mircea. *Images and Symbols: Studies in Religious Symbolism*. 1952. Princeton, NJ: Princeton University Press, 1991 ed.

———. *The Sacred and the Profane: The Nature of Religion* (Willard R. Trask, trans.). 1957. San Diego, CA: Harvest, 1959 ed.

———. *A History of Religious Ideas: From Gautama Buddha to the Triumph of Christianity* (Willard R. Trask, trans.). Vol. 2. 1978. Chicago, IL: University of Chicago Press, 1982 ed.

Eliot, Alexander. *The Universal Myths: Heroes, Gods, Tricksters, and Others*. New York, NY: Meridian, 1976.

Elliot, Neil. *Sensuality in Scandinavia*. New York, NY: Weybright and Talley, 1970.

Ellis, Peter Berresford. *A Dictionary of Irish Mythology*. 1987. Oxford, UK: Oxford University Press, 1992 ed.

Elton, Charles Isaac. *Origins of English History*. London, UK: Bernard Quaritch, 1890.

Encyclopedia Britannica: A New Survey of Universal Knowledge. 1768. Chicago, IL/London, UK: Encyclopedia Britannica, 1955 ed.

Eusebius (of Caesarea). *The History of the Church* (G. A. Williamson, trans; Andrew Louth, ed.). Circa C.E. 315-325. Harmondsworth, UK: Penguin, 1965 (1989 ed.).

Evans, Bergen. *Dictionary of Mythology*. 1970. New York, NY: Laurel,

1991 ed.

Evans, Elizabeth Edson. *The Christ Myth: A Study*. New York, NY: Truth Seeker Co., 1900.

Farmer, David Hugh. *The Oxford Dictionary of Saints*. 1978. Oxford, UK: Oxford University Press, 1992 ed.

Farrell, Deborah, and Carole Presser (eds.). *The Herder Symbol Dictionary: Symbols from Art, Archaeology, Mythology, Literature, and Religion* (Boris Matthews, trans.). 1978. Wilmette, IL: Chiron, 1990 ed.

Ferguson, George. *Signs and Symbols in Christian Art*. 1954. London, UK: Oxford University Press, 1975 ed.

Feuerstein, Georg. *Sacred Sexuality: Living the Vision of the Erotic Spirit*. 1992. New York, NY: Tarcher, 1993 ed.

Fideler, David. *Jesus Christ, Sun of God: Ancient Cosmology and Early Christian Symbolism*. Wheaton, IL: Quest, 1993.

Fillmore, Charles, and Theodosia DeWitt Schobert. *Metaphysical Bible Dictionary*. Unity Village, MO: Unity School of Christianity, 1931.

Finegan, Jack. *Light from the Ancient Past: The Archaeological Background of the Hebrew-Christian Religion* (Vol. 1). 1946. Princeton, NJ: Princeton University Press, 1974 ed.

Finger, Ben, Jr. *Concise World History*. New York, NY: Philosophical Library, 1959.

Fischer, Carl. *The Myth and Legend of Greece*. Dayton, OH: George A. Pflaum, 1968.

Ford, Guy Stanton (ed.-in-chief). *Compton's Pictured Encyclopedia*. 1922. Chicago: F. E. Compton and Co., 1957 ed.

Forrest, M. Isidora. *Offering to Isis: Knowing the Goddess Through Her Sacred Symbols*. St. Paul, MN: Llewellyn, 2005.

Fox, Matthew. *The Coming of the Cosmic Christ : The Healing of Mother Earth and the Birth of a Global Renaissance*. New York, NY: Harper and Row, 1988.

Fox, Robin Lane. *Pagans and Christians*. New York, NY: Knopf, 1986.

———. *The Unauthorized Version: Truth and Fiction in the Bible.* New York, NY: Knopf, 1991.

Frazer, Sir James George. *The Golden Bough: A Study in Magic and Religion.* 1922. New York, NY: Collier, 1963 (abridged) ed.

———. *Folklore in the Old Testament.* New York, NY: Tudor Publishing, (abridged) 1923.

Freke, Timothy, and Peter Grandy. *The Jesus Mysteries: Was the Original Jesus a Pagan God?* New York, NY: Three Rivers Press, 1999.

———. *Jesus and the Lost Goddess: The Secret Teachings of the Original Christians.* New York, NY: Three Rivers Press, 2002.

Freud, Sigmund. *Totem and Taboo.* 1918. New York, NY: Vintage, 1946 ed.

———. *The Future of an Illusion.* 1928. New York, NY: W. W. Norton, 1961 ed.

———. *New Introductory Lectures Psychoanalysis.* Lecture no. 35: "A Philosophy of Life," 1932.

Gantz, Jeffrey (trans.). *Early Irish Myths and Sagas.* 1981. Harmondsworth, UK: Penguin, 1988 ed.

Gaskell, G. A. *Dictionary of All Scriptures and Myths.* 1960. New York, NY: Julian Press, 1973 ed.

Gelling, Peter, and Hilda Ellis Davidson. *The Chariot of the Sun and Other Rites and Symbols of the Northern Bronze Age.* New York, NY: Frederick A. Praeger, 1969.

Gimbutas, Marija Alseikait. *The Goddesses and Gods of Old Europe: Myths and Cult Images.* 1974. Berkeley, CA: University of California Press, 1992 ed.

———. *The Civilization of the Goddess: The World of Old Europe* (Joan Marler, ed.). New York, NY: HarperCollins, 1991.

Glyn, Anthony. *The British: Portrait of a People.* New York, NY: G. P. Putnam's Sons, 1970.

Goldenberg, Naomi. *The Changing of the Gods: Feminism and the End of Traditional Religions.* Boston, MA: Beacon Press, 1979.

Gordon, Richard Stuart. *The Encyclopedia of Myths and Legends.* 1993. London, UK: Headline, 1994 ed.

Goring, Rosemary (ed.). *Larousse Dictionary of Beliefs and Religions.* 1992. Edinburgh, Scotland: Larousse, 1995 ed.

Graham, Lloyd M. *Deceptions and Myths of the Bible.* 1975. New York, NY: Citadel Press, 1990 ed.

Grant, Michael, and John Hazel. *Who's Who in Classical Mythology.* 1973. New York, NY: Oxford University Press, 1993 ed.

Graves, Kersey. *The World's Sixteen Crucified Saviors, or, Christianity Before Christianity: Containing New, Startling, and Extraordinary Revelations in Religious History, which Disclose the Oriental Origin of All the Doctrines, Principles, Precepts, and Miracles of the Christian New Testament, and Furnishing a Key for Unlocking Many of Its Sacred Mysteries, Besides Comprising the History of Sixteen Heathen Crucified Gods.* Boston, MA: Colby and Rich, 1876.

Graves, Robert. *The White Goddess: A Historical Grammar of Poetic Myth.* 1948. New York, NY: Noonday Press, 1991 ed.

——. *The Greek Myths.* 1955. Harmondsworth, UK: Penguin, 1992 combined ed.

Graves, Robert, and Raphael Patai. *Hebrew Myths: The Book of Genesis.* 1964. New York, NY: Anchor, 1989 ed.

Gray, John. *Near Eastern Mythology: Mesopotamia, Syria, and Palestine.* London, UK: Hamlyn, 1963.

Green, John Richard. *A Short History of the English People* (Vol. 1). London, UK: Macmillan and Co., 1892.

Greenberg, Gary. *The Bible Myth: The African Origins of the Jewish People.* Secaucus, NJ: Citadel Press, 1996.

——. *101 Myths of the Bible: How Ancient Scribes Invented Biblical History.* Naperville, IL: Sourcebooks, 2000.

Grimal, Pierre. *The Penguin Dictionary of Classical Mythology* (A. R. Maxwell-Hyslop, trans.). 1951. Harmondsworth, UK: Penguin, 1990 ed.

Grotjahn, Martin. *The Voice of the Symbol*. Los Angeles, CA: Mara Books, 1971.

Gruss, Edmond C. *What Every Mormon Should Know*. 1975. Denver, CO: Accent, 1976 ed.

Guignebert, Charles. *The Christ*. 1943. New York, NY: Citadel, 1968 ed.

Guthrie, William K. C. *The Greeks and Their Gods*. Boston, MA: Beacon Press, 1955.

Hadas, Moses (ed.). *A History of Rome*. Garden City, NY: Doubleday Anchor, 1956.

Haining, Peter. *Witchcraft and Black Magic*. New York, NY: Grosset and Dunlap, 1972.

Hall, Eleanor L. *The Moon and the Virgin: Reflections on the Archetypal Feminine*. New York, NY: Harper and Row, 1980.

Hall, John Richard Clark. *A Concise Anglo-Saxon Dictionary*. 1894. Toronto, Canada: University of Toronto Press (and the Medieval Academy of America), 1960 ed. (1996 imprint).

Hall, Manly P. *The Secret Teachings of All Ages*. 1925. Los Angeles, CA: The Philosophical Research Society, 1989 ed.

Halliday, William Reginald. *Greek and Roman Folklore*. New York, NY: Cooper Square, 1963.

Hamilton, Edith. *The Greek Way*. 1930. New York, NY: Mentor, 1959 ed.

——. *The Roman Way*. 1932. New York, NY: Mentor, 1961 ed.

——. *Mythology: Timeless Tales of Gods and Heroes*. 1940. New York, NY: Mentor, 1963 ed.

Hardon, John A. *Pocket Catholic Dictionary*. 1980. New York, NY: Image, 1985 ed.

Harrison, Michael. *The Roots of Witchcraft*. Secaucus, NJ: Citadel Press, 1974.

Haskins, Susan. *Mary Magdalene: Myth and Metaphor*. New York, NY: Harcourt Brace and Co., 1993.

Heidel, Alexander. *The Gilgamesh Epic and Old Testament Parallels*. Chicago, IL: University of Chicago Press, 1949.

Heindel, Max. *Nature Spirits and Nature Forces*. Oceanside, CA: Rosicrucian Fellowship, 1937.

Herm, Gerhard. *The Celts: The People Who Came Out of the Darkness*. New York, NY: St. Martin's Press, 1976.

Hinnells, John R. (ed.). *Persian Mythology*. London, UK: Hamlyn, 1973.

——. *The Penguin Dictionary of Religions: From Abraham to Zoroaster*. 1984. Harmondsworth, UK: Penguin, 1986 ed.

Hodson, Geoffrey. *The Hidden Wisdom in the Holy Bible*. Vol. 1. 1967. Wheaton, IL: Quest/Theosophical Publishing House, 1978 ed.

——. *The Hidden Wisdom in the Holy Bible*. Vol. 2. 1967. Wheaton, IL: Quest/Theosophical Publishing House, 1978 ed.

Hoeller, Stephan A. *Jung and the Lost Gospels: Insights into the Dead Sea Scrolls and the Nag Hammadi Library*. 1989. Wheaton, IL: Quest, 1990 ed.

Holroyd, Stuart. *The Arkana Dictionary of New Perspectives*. Harmondsworth, UK: Arkana, 1989.

Hooke, S. K. *Middle Eastern Mythology: From the Assyrians to the Hebrews*. 1963. Harmondsworth, UK: Penguin, 1991 ed.

Hopfe, Lewis M. *Religions of the World*. 1976. New York, NY: Macmillan, 1987 ed.

Hoyland, Robert G. *Arabia and the Arabs: From the Bronze Age to the Coming of Islam*. London, UK: Routledge, 2001.

Hutchinson, Richard Wyatt. *Prehistoric Crete*. 1962. Harmondsworth, UK: Penguin, 1968 ed.

Hutton, Ronald. *The Pagan Religions of the Ancient British Isles: Their Nature and Legacy*. 1991. Oxford, UK: Blackwell, 2000 ed.

Huxley, Francis. *The Way of the Sacred*. New York, NY: Doubleday, 1974.

Ide, Arthur Frederick. *Yahweh's Wife: Sex in the Evolution of Monotheism*. Las Colinas, TX: Monument Press, 1991.

Jabbar, Mailk H. *The Astrological Foundation of the Christ Myth*. 4 vols.

Dayton, OH: Rare Books Distributor, 1995-2003.

Jackson, John G. *Christianity Before Christ*. Austin, TX: American Atheist Press, 1985.

James, Peter, and Nick Thorpe. *Ancient Inventions*. New York, NY: Ballantine, 1994.

Johns, June. *Black Magic Today*. London, UK: New English Library, 1971.

Johnson, B. *The Gods and Goddesses of Classical Mythology: Being a Short Classical Dictionary*. London, UK: W. Stewart and Co., 1882.

Johnson, Robert A. *She: Understanding Feminine Psychology*. 1976. New York, NY: Perennial, 1977 ed.

Johnson, Walter, and William Wright. *Neolithic Man in North-East Surrey*. London, UK: Elliot Stock, 1903.

Jonas, Hans. *The Gnostic Religion: The Message of the Alien God and the Beginnings of Christianity*. 1958. Boston, MA: Beacon Press, 2001 ed.

Jones, Gwyn. *A History of the Vikings*. 1968. Oxford, UK: Oxford University Press, 1984 ed.

Jones, Prudence, and Nigel Pennick. *A History of Pagan Europe*. London, UK: Routledge, 1995.

Josephus: Complete Works (William Whiston, trans.). Circa 1st to 2nd Centuries A.D. 1960. Grand Rapids, MI: Kregel Publications, 1980 ed.

Julian of Norwich. *Revelations of Divine Love*. 1373. Harmondsworth, UK: Penguin, 1966 ed.

Jung, Carl Gustav. *Man and His Symbols*. 1964. New York, NY: Dell, 1968 ed.

Keller, Werner. *The Bible As History: A Confirmation of the Book of Books* (William Neil, trans.). 1956. New York, NY: Bantam, 1980 ed.

Kelly, Sean, and Rosemary Rogers. *Saints Preserve Us!: Everything You Need to Know About Every Saint You'll Ever Need*. New York, NY: Randon House, 1993.

Kelsey, Morton T., and Barbara Kelsey. *Sacrament of Sexuality: The*

Spirituality and Psychology of Sex. Warwick, NY: Amity House, 1986.

Kinsley, David. *The Goddesses' Mirror: Visions of the Divine From East and West*. Albany, NY: State University of New York Press, 1989.

Kirk, G. S. *The Nature of the Greek Myths*. 1974. Harmondsworth, UK: Penguin, 1978 ed.

Klein, Peter (ed.). *The Catholic Source Book*. Dubuque, IA: Brown-Roa, 2000.

Knight, Richard Payne. *A Discourse On the Worship of Priapus, and Its Connection With the Mystic Theology of the Ancients*. London, UK: privately printed, 1865 ed.

——. *The Symbolic Language of Ancient Art and Mythology*. New York, NY: J. W. Bouton, 1892.

Knight, Sirona. *Exploring Celtic Druidism: Ancient Magick and Rituals for Personal Empowerment*. Franklin Lakes, NJ: Career Press, 2001.

Koran, The (George Sale, trans.). 1734. London, UK: Frederick Warne and Co. Ltd., n.d.

Kramarae, Cheris, and Paula A. Treichler. *A Feminist Dictionary*. Champaign, IL: University of Illinois Press, 1996.

Kramer, Heinrich, and Jakob Sprenger. *Malleus Maleficarum*. 1486. New York, NY: Dover, 1971.

Kramer, Samuel Noah. *History Begins at Sumer: Thirty-Nine Firsts in Recorded History*. 1956. Philadelphia, PA: University of Pennsylvania Press, 1981 ed.

Kuhn, Alvin Boyd. *A Rebirth For Christianity*. 1970. Wheaton, IL: Quest, 2005.

Lacy, Norris J. (ed.). *The Arthurian Encyclopedia*. New York, NY: Garland Publishing, 1986.

Laistner, Max Ludwig Wolfram. *Christianity and Pagan Culture in the Later Roman Empire*. Ithaca, NY: Cornell University Press, 1951.

Lamsa, George M. *The Holy Bible: From Ancient Eastern Manuscripts*. 1933. Philadelphia, PA: A. J. Holman, 1968 ed.

Larousse Encyclopedia of Mythology, New. 1959. London, UK: Hamlyn, 1976 ed.

Lass, Abraham H., David Kiremidjian, and Ruth M. Goldstein. *The Dictionary of Classical, Biblical, and Literary Allusions.* New York, NY: Fawcett Gold Medal, 1987.

LaVey, Anton Szandor. *The Satanic Bible.* New York, NY: Avon, 1969.

Layton, Bentley. *The Gnostic Scriptures: Ancient Wisdom for the New Age.* 1987. New York, NY: Anchor, 1995 ed.

Leakey, Richard E., and Roger Lewin. *Origins Reconsidered: In Search of What Makes Us Human.* New York, NY: Doubleday, 1992.

Leeming, David Adams. *The World of Myth.* 1990. Oxford, UK: Oxford University Press, 1992 ed.

——. *Jealous Gods and Chosen People: The Mythology of the Middle East.* New York, NY: Oxford University Press, 2004.

Legge, Francis. *Forerunners and Rivals of Christianity.* 2 vols. New York, NY: University Books, 1964.

LeLoup, Jean-Yves. *The Gospel of Mary Magdalene.* Rochester, VT: Inner Traditions, 2002.

——. *The Gospel of Philip: Jesus, Mary Magdalene, and the Gnosis of Sacred Union.* Rochester, VT: Inner Traditions, 2004.

——. *The Gospel of Thomas: The Gnostic Wisdom of Jesus.* Rochester, VT: Inner Traditions, 2005.

Lerner, Gerda. *The Creation of Patriarchy.* 1986. Oxford, UK: Oxford University Press, 1987 ed.

Levi. *The Aquarian Gospel of Jesus the Christ: The Philosophic and Practical Basis of the Religion of the Aquarian Age of the World and of the Church Universal.* Marina Del Ray, CA: DeVorss and Co., 1982.

Lewis, Harvey Spencer. *Mansions of the Soul: The Cosmic Conception.* 1930. San Jose, CA: Ancient Mystical Order Rosae Crucis (AMORC), 1969 ed.

Lilly, William. *Christian Astrology.* 3 vols. 1647. New York, NY: Cosimo, 2005 ed.

Lindsay, Jack. *The Origins of Astrology*. New York, NY: Barnes and Noble, 1971.

Littleton, C. Scott (ed). *Mythology: The Illustrated Anthology of World Myth and Storytelling*. London, UK: Duncan Baird Publishers, 2002.

Lockyer, Herbert. *All the Women of the Bible*. Grand Rapids, MI: Zondervan, n.d.

Loetscher, Lefferts A. (ed.-in-chief). *Twentieth Century Encyclopedia of Religious Knowledge*. 2 vols. Grand Rapids, MI: Baker Book House, 1955.

Lost Books of the Bible and the Forgotten Books of Eden, The. Iowa Falls, IA: World Bible Publishers, 1926.

Luckey, Thomas D. *Radiation Hormesis*. Boca Raton, FL: CRC Press, 1991.

Ludlow, Daniel H. (ed.). *Encyclopedia of Mormonism: The History, Scripture, Doctrine, and Procedure of the Church of Jesus Christ of Latter-Day Saints*. New York, NY: Macmillan, 1992.

Lurker, Manfred. *The Gods and Symbols of Ancient Egypt*. 1974. New York, NY: Thames and Hudson, 1984 ed.

———. *Dictionary of Gods and Goddesses, Devils and Demons* (G. L. Campbell, trans.). 1984. London, UK: Routledge, 1988 ed.

MacCana, Proinsias. *Celtic Mythology*. London, UK: Hamlyn, 1970.

MacLysaght, Edward. *The Surnames of Ireland*. 1985. Dublin, Ireland: Irish Academic Press, 1999 ed.

Malachi, Tau. *Gnosis of the Cosmic Christ: A Gnostic Christian Kabbalah*. St. Paul, MN: Llewellyn, 2005.

———. *Living Gnosis: A Practical Guide to Gnostic Christianity*. St. Paul, MN: Llewellyn, 2005.

———. *St. Mary Magdalene: The Gnostic Tradition of the Holy Bride*. St. Paul, MN: Llewellyn, 2006.

Mann, Nicholas R. *The Isle of Avalon: Sacred Mysteries of Arthur and Glastonbury*. London, UK: Green Magic, 2001.

Marcus, Rebecca B. *Prehistoric Cave Paintings*. New York, NY: Franklin

Watts, 1968.

Markale, Jean. *Cathedral of the Black Madonna: The Druids and the Mysteries of Chartres*. Rochester, VT: Inner Traditions, 2004.

Maspero, Gaston. *Popular Stories of Ancient Egypt*. New York, NY: University Books, 1967.

Massey, Gerald. *The Historical Jesus, and the Mythical Christ: Natural Genesis and Typology of Equinoctial Christolatry*. 1883. New York, NY: Cosimo, 2006 ed.

——. *Ancient Egypt: The Light of the World*. 12 vols. London, UK: T. Fisher Unwin, 1907.

Matthews, Caitlín and John. *The Encyclopedia of Celtic Wisdom: A Celtic Shaman's Sourcebook*. Rockport, MA: Element, 1994.

Matthews, John. *The Winter Solstice: The Sacred Traditions of Christmas*. Wheaton, IL: Quest, 2003.

McArthur, Tom (ed.). *The Oxford Companion to the English Language*. Oxford, UK: Oxford University Press, 1992.

McConkie, Bruce R. *Mormon Doctrine*. 1966. Salt Lake City, UT: Bookcraft, 1992 ed.

McKenzie, John L. *Dictionary of the Bible*. New York, NY: Collier, 1965.

McKinsey, C. Dennis. *The Encyclopedia of Biblical Errancy*. Amherst, NY: Prometheus, 1995.

McLean, Adam (ed.). *A Treatise on Angel Magic: Magnum Opus Hermetic Sourceworks*. 1989. York Beach, ME: Weiser, 2006 ed.

Mead, George Robert Stow. *Thrice-Greatest Hermes: Studies in Hellenistic Theosophy and Gnosis*. London, UK: Theosophical Publishing Society, 1906.

——. *The Mysteries of Mithra*. London, UK: Theosophical Publishing Society, 1907.

Mead, Frank Spencer, and Samuel S. Hill. *Handbook of Denominations in the United States*. 1951. Nashville, TN: Abingdon Press, 1989 ed.

Mead, Margaret. *Male and Female: A Study of the Sexes in a Changing World*. 1955. New York, NY: Mentor, 1959 ed.

Meredith, Joel. *Meredith's Book of Bible Lists*. Minneapolis, MN: Bethany House, 1980.

Metford, J. C. J. *Dictionary of Christian Lore and Legend*. London, UK: Thames and Hudson, 1983.

Metzger, Bruce M., and Michael D. Coogan (eds.). *The Oxford Companion to the Bible*. New York, NY: Oxford University Press, 1993.

Meurois-Givaudan, Anne and Daniel. *The Way of the Essenes: Christ's Hidden Life Remembered*. Rochester, VT: Destiny, 1992.

Miller, Malcolm. *Chartres Cathedral*. New York, NY: Riverside Book Co., 1997.

Mills, A. D. *Oxford Dictionary of English Place-names*. 1991. Oxford, UK: Oxford University Press, 1998 ed.

Mish, Frederick (ed.). *Webster's Ninth New Collegiate Dictionary*. Springfield, MA: Merriam-Webster, 1984 ed.

Mollenkott, Virginia Ramey. *The Divine Feminine: The Biblical Imagery of God as Female*. New York, NY: Crossroad Publishing, 1993.

Monaghan, Patricia. *The Book of Goddesses and Heroines*. 1990. St. Paul, MN: Llewellyn, 1991 ed.

Monroe, Douglas. *The 21 Lessons of Merlyn: A Study in Druid Magic and Lore*. St. Paul, MN: Llewellyn, 1992.

Montagu, Ashley. *The Natural Superiority of Women*. 1952. New York, NY: Collier, 1992 ed.

Morehead, Albert H. (ed.). *The Illustrated World Encyclopedia*. 1954. Woodbury, NY: Bobley Publishing, 1977 ed.

Morgan, Elaine. *The Descent of Woman*. 1972. New York, NY: Bantam, 1973 ed.

Nelson, Thomas (pub.). *Nelson's New Compact Illustrated Bible Dictionary*. 1964. Nashville, TN: Thomas Nelson, 1978 ed.

Neumann, Erich. *The Great Mother: An Analysis of the Archetype* (Ralph Manheim, trans.). New York, NY: Pantheon, 1955.

Newall, Venetia. *The Encyclopedia of Witchcraft and Magic*. New York, NY: A and W Visual Library, 1974.

Norton-Taylor, Duncan. *The Emergence of Man: The Celts*. New York, NY: Time-Life, 1974.

O'Brien, Arthur. *Europe Before Modern Times: An Ancient and Medieval History*. 1940. Chicago, IL: Loyola University Press, 1943 ed.

Odent, Michael. *Water and Sexuality*. Harmondsworth, UK: Arkana, 1990.

O'Flaherty, Wendy Doniger. *Hindu Myths*. Harmondsworth, UK: Penguin, 1975.

Olson, Carl (ed.). *The Book of the Goddess, Past and Present: An Introduction to Her Religion*. New York, NY: Crossroad, 1983.

Orme, A. R. *Ireland* (from "The World's Landscapes" series, James M. Houston, ed). Chicago, IL: Aldine, 1970.

Osborne, John. *Britain*. New York, NY: Time-Life, 1963.

Oxford English Dictionary, The (compact edition, 2 vols.). 1928. Oxford, UK: Oxford University Press, 1979 ed.

Pagels, Elaine. *The Gnostic Gospels*. 1979. New York, NY: Vintage, 1981 ed.

——. *Adam, Eve, and the Serpent*. 1988. New York, NY: Vintage, 1989 ed.

——. *The Origin of Satan*. New York, NY: Random House, 1995.

Patai, Raphael. *The Hebrew Goddess*. 1967. Detroit, MI: Wayne State University Press, 1990 ed.

Paulsen, Kathryn. *The Complete Book of Magic and Witchcraft*. 1970. New York, NY: Signet, 1980 ed.

Pearson, Carol S. *Awakening the Heroes Within: Twelve Archetypes to Help Us Find Ourselves and Transform Our World*. New York, NY: HarperCollins, 1991.

Pennick, Nigel. *The Pagan Book of Days: A Guide to the Festivals, Traditions, and Sacred Days of the Year*. Rochester, VT: Destiny, 1992.

Pepper, Elizabeth, and John Wilcock. *Magical and Mystical Sites: Europe and the British Isles*. Grand Rapids, MI: Phanes Press, 1992.

Perowne, Stewart. *Roman Mythology*. 1969. Twickenham, UK: Newnes Books, 1986 ed.

Pinch, Geraldine. *Egyptian Mythology: A Guide to the Gods, Goddesses, and Traditions of Ancient Egypt*. Oxford, UK: Oxford University Press, 2004.

Prahbupada, A. C. Bhaktivedanta Swami. *Beyond Birth and Death*. Los Angeles, CA: The Bhaktivedanta Book Trust, 1979.

Prophet, Elizabeth Clare. *Mary Magdalene and the Divine Feminine: Jesus' Lost Teachings on Woman - How Orthodoxy Suppressed Jesus' Revolution for Woman and Invented Original Sin*. Gardiner, MT: Summit University Press, 2005.

Qualls-Corbett, Nancy. *The Sacred Prostitute: Eternal Aspect of the Feminine*. Toronto, Canada: Inner City Books, 1988.

Raftery, Barry. *Pagan Celtic Ireland: The Enigma of the Irish Iron Age*. London, UK: Thames and Hudson, 1994.

Ramm, Bernard L. *Hermeneutics*. 1967. Grand Rapids, MI: Baker Book House, 1988 ed.

Reaney, P. H., and R. M. Wilson. *A Dictionary of English Surnames*. 1958. Oxford, UK: Oxford University Press, 1997 ed.

Reed, Ellen Cannon. *Circle of Isis: Ancient Egyptian Magic for Modern Witches*. Franklin Lakes, NJ: Career Press, 2002.

Regula, deTraci. *The Mysteries of Isis: Her Worship and Magick*. 1995. St. Paul, MN: Llewellyn, 2001 ed.

Reilly, Patricia Lynn. *A God Who Looks Like Me: Discovering a Woman-Affirming Spirituality*. New York, NY: Ballantine, 1995.

Roberts, R. Philip. *Mormonism Unmasked: Confronting the Contradictions Between Mormon Beliefs and True Christianity*. Nashville, TN: Broadman and Holman, 1998.

Robertson, John M. *Christianity and Mythology*. London, UK: Watts and Co., 1900.

——. *A Short History of Christianity*. London, UK: Watts and Co., 1902.

——. *Pagan Christs: Studies in Comparative Hierology*. London, UK: Watts and Co., 1903.

——. *Pagan Christs*. 1966. New York, NY: Dorset Press, 1987 ed.

Robinson, James M (ed.). *The Nag Hammadi Library in English.* 1978. San Francisco, CA: Harper Collins, 1990 ed.

Rocco, Sha. *Sex Mythology.* 1898. Austin, TX: American Atheist Press, 1982 ed.

Rufus, Anneli S., and Kristan Lawson. *Goddess Sites: Europe.* New York, NY: HarperCollins, 1991.

Runciman, Steven. *A History of the Crusades: Vol. 1, The First Crusade and the Foundation of the Kingdom of Jerusalem.* 1951. New York, NY: Harper Torchbooks, 1964 ed.

Runes, Dagobert D. (ed.). *Dictionary of Judaism.* 1959. New York, NY: Citadel Press, 1991 ed.

Russell, Bertrand. *Why I Am Not a Christian: and Other Essays on Religion and Related Subjects.* New York, NY: Touchstone, 1957.

Rutherford, Ward. *Celtic Mythology: The Nature and Influence of Celtic Myth—From Druidism to Arthurian Legend.* New York, NY: Sterling, 1990.

Salmonson, Jessica Amanda. *The Encyclopedia of Amazons: Women Warriors from Antiquity to the Modern Era.* New York, NY: Paragon House, 1991.

Schwartz, Howard. *Gabriel's Palace: Jewish Mystical Tales.* New York, NY: Oxford University Press, 1993.

——. *Tree of Souls: The Mythology of Judaism.* Oxford, UK: Oxford University Press, 2004.

Scott, George Ryley. *Phallic Worship: A History of Sex and Sexual Rites.* London, UK: Senate, 1996.

Seabrook, Lochlainn. *Aphrodite's Trade: The Hidden History of Prostitution Unveiled.* 1993. Franklin, TN: Sea Raven Press, 2020 ed.

——. *Britannia Rules: Goddess-Worship in Ancient Anglo-Celtic Society - An Academic Look at the United Kingdom's Spiritual Matricentric Past.* 1999. Franklin, TN: Sea Raven Press, 2010 ed.

——. *The Book of Kelle: An Introduction to Goddess-Worship and the Great Celtic Mother-Goddess Kelle, Original Blessed Lady of Ireland.* 1999.

Franklin, TN: Sea Raven Press, 2010 ed.

———. *The Caudills: An Etymological, Ethnological, and Genealogical Study - Exploring the Name and National Origins of a European-American Family*. 2003. Franklin, TN: Sea Raven Press, 2010 ed.

———. *Carnton Plantation Ghost Stories: True Tales of the Unexplained from Tennessee's Most Haunted Civil War House!* 2005. Franklin, TN, 2016 ed.

———. *The McGavocks of Carnton Plantation: A Southern History - Celebrating One of Dixie's Most Noble Confederate Families and Their Tennessee Home*. 2008. Franklin, TN, 2011 ed.

———. *Abraham Lincoln: The Southern View - Demythologizing America's Sixteenth President*. Franklin, TN: Sea Raven Press, 2009.

———. *Christmas Before Christianity: How the Birthday of the "Sun" Became the Birthday of the "Son."* Franklin, TN: Sea Raven Press, 2010.

———. *Jesus and the Law of Attraction: The Bible-Based Guide to Creating Perfect Health, Wealth, and Happiness Following Christ's Simple Formula*. Franklin, TN: Sea Raven Press, 2013.

———. *The Bible and the Law of Attraction: 99 Teachings of Jesus, the Apostles, and the Prophets*. Franklin, TN: Sea Raven Press, 2013.

———. *Christ Is All and In All: Rediscovering Your Divine Nature and the Kingdom Within*. Franklin, TN: Sea Raven Press, 2014.

———. *Jesus and the Gospel of Q: Christ's Pre-Christian Teachings as Recorded in the New Testament*. 2014. Spring Hill, TN: Sea Raven Press, 2020 ed.

———. *Seabrook's Bible Dictionary of Traditional and Mystical Christian Doctrines*. Spring Hill, TN: Sea Raven Press, 2016.

———. *The Way of Holiness: The Evolution of Religion—From the Cave Bear Cult to Christianity*. Franklin, TN: Sea Raven Press, unpublished manuscript.

———. *The Goddess Encyclopedia of Secret Words, Names, and Places*. Franklin, TN: Sea Raven Press, unpublished manuscript.

———. *Seabrook's Complete Encyclopedia of Deities*. Franklin, TN: Sea Raven

Press, unpublished manuscript.
——. *The Unauthorized Encyclopedia of the Bible*. Franklin, TN: Sea Raven Press, unpublished manuscript.
——. *The Complete Dictionary of Christian Mythology*. Franklin, TN: Sea Raven Press, unpublished manuscript.
Seznec, Jean. *The Survival of the Pagan Gods*. Princeton, NJ: Princeton University Press, 1953.
Shah, Amina. *Arabian Fairy Tales*. London, UK: Octagon Press, 1989.
——. *Tales From the Bazaars of Arabia: Folk Stories From the Middle East*. London, UK: Octagon Press, 2002.
Shaw, Ian (ed.). *The Oxford History of Ancient Egypt*. 2000. Oxford, UK: Oxford University Press, 2002 ed.
Sherfey, Mary Jane. *The Nature and Evolution of Female Sexuality*. 1972. New York, NY: Vintage, 1973 ed.
Simons, Gerald. *Barbarian Europe* (from the *Great Ages of Man* series). New York, NY: Time-Life, 1968.
Sjöö, Monica, and Barbara Mor. *The Great Cosmic Mother: Rediscovering the Religion of the Earth*. New York, NY: Harper and Row, 1987.
Skelton, Robin, and Margaret Blackwood. *Earth, Air, Fire, Water: Pre-Christian and Pagan Elements in British Songs, Rhymes and Ballads*. Harmondsworth, UK: Arkana, 1990.
Smith, Lacey Baldwin. *This Realm of England: 1399 to 1688*. 1966. Lexington, MA: D. C. Heath and Co., 1983 ed.
Smith, William. *Smith's Bible Dictionary*. Circa 1880s. Nashville, TN: Thomas Nelson, 1986 ed.
Sobol, Donald J. *The Amazons of Greek Mythology*. Cranbury, NJ: A.S. Barnes and Co., 1972.
Spence, Lewis. *Ancient Egyptian Myths and Legends*. 1915. New York, NY: Dover, 1990 ed.
——. *An Encyclopedia of Occultism*. 1920. New York, NY: Citadel Press, 1993 ed.
——. *The History and Origins of Druidism*. 1949. New York, NY: Samuel

Weiser, 1971 ed.

Starbird, Margaret. *The Goddess in the Gospels: Reclaiming the Sacred Feminine.* Rochester, VT: Bear and Co., 1998.

——. *Magdalene's Lost Legacy: Symbolic Numbers and the Sacred Union in Christianity.* Rochester, VT: Bear and Co., 2003.

Stark, Rodney. *Discovering God: The Origins of the Great Religions and the Evolution of Belief.* New York, NY: HarperCollins, 2007.

Stein, Diane. *The Goddess Book of Days.* 1988. Freedom, CA: The Crossing Press, 1992 ed.

Stetkevych, Jaroslav. *Muhammad and the Golden Bough: Reconstructing Arabian Myth.* Bloomington, IN: Indiana University Press, 1996.

Stone, Merlin. *When God was a Woman.* San Diego, CA: Harvest, 1976.

——. *Ancient Mirrors of Womanhood: A Treasury of Goddess and Heroine Lore from Around the World.* 1979. Boston, MA: Beacon Press, 1990 ed.

Strachan, Gordon. *Chartres: Sacred Geometry, Sacred Space.* Edinburgh, Scotland: Floris Books, 2003.

Streep, Peg. *Sanctuaries of the Goddess: The Sacred Landscapes and Objects.* Boston, MA: Bullfinch Press, 1994.

Strieber, Whitley. *Communion: A True Story.* New York, NY: Avon, 1987.

——. *Transformation: The Breakthrough.* New York, NY: Avon, 1997.

——. *Confirmation: The Hard Evidence of Aliens Among Us.* New York, NY: St. Martin's Press, 1998.

Strong, James. *Strong's Exhaustive Concordance of the Bible.* 1890. Nashville, TN: Abingdon Press, 1975 ed.

Sturluson, Snorri. *The Prose Edda.* Berkeley, CA: University of California Press, 1954.

Swindoll, Cynthia (ed.). *Abraham: Friend of God.* 1986. Fullerton, CA: Insight for Living, 1988 ed.

Sykes, Egerton. *Who's Who in Non-Classical Mythology.* 1952. New York, NY: Oxford University Press, 1993 ed.

Szekely, Edmond Bordeaux. *The Essene Gospel of Peace.* 1937. Nelson,

B.C., Canada: International Biogenic Society, 1981 ed.

Telushkin, Rabbi Joseph. *Jewish Literacy*. New York, NY: William Morrow and Co., 1991.

Tenney, Merrill C. (gen. ed.). *Handy Dictionary of the Bible*. Grand Rapids, MI: Lamplighter, 1965.

The Epic of Gilgamesh (N. K. Sandars, ed.). Circa 3000 B.C. Harmondsworth, UK: Penguin, 1960 (1972 ed.).

The Fossil Record and Evolution. Collected articles from *Scientific American*. San Francisco, CA: W. H. Freeman and Co., 1982 ed.

The Golden Treasury of Myths and Legends (adapted by Anne Terry White). New York, NY: Golden Press, 1959.

The Journal of Hellenic Studies. Vol. 7. London, UK: Society for the Promotion of Hellenic Studies, 1886.

Thompson Chain-Reference Bible, The. King James Version. Indianapolis: B. B. Kirkbride Bible Co., 1964.

Thompson, James Westfall, and Edgar Nathaniel Johnson. *An Introduction to Medieval Europe: 300-1500*. New York, NY: W. W. Norton, 1937.

Thorsten, Geraldine. *God Herself: The Feminine Roots of Astrology*. New York, NY: Avon, 1981.

Tompkins, Peter. *Secrets of the Great Pyramid*. 1971. New York, NY: Harper Colophon, 1978 ed.

Towns, Elmer L. *The Names of Jesus*. Denver, CO: Accent, 1987.

Traupman, John C. *The New College Latin and English Dictionary*. 1966. New York, NY: Bantam, 1988 ed.

——. *The Bantam New College German and English Dictionary*. 1981. New York, NY: Bantam, 1986 ed.

Trevelyan, George Macaulay. *History of England: Vol. 1, From the Earliest Times to the Reformation*. 1926. Garden City, NY: Anchor, 1952 ed.

Tripp, Edward. *History of England: Vol. 2, The Tudors and the Stuart Era*. 1926. Garden City, NY: Anchor, 1952 ed.

———. *The Meridian Handbook of Classical Mythology*. 1970. Harmondsworth, UK: Meridian, 1974 ed.

Turcan, Robert. *The Cults of the Roman Empire*. 1992. Oxford, UK: Blackwell, 2000 ed.

Udry, J. Richard. *The Social Context of Marriage*. 1966. Philadelphia, PA: J. B. Lippincott, 1974 ed.

Van De Mieroop, Marc. *A History of the Ancient Near East, ca. 3000-323 BC*. 2004. Oxford, UK: Blackwell, 2007 ed.

Vermaseren, Maarten J. *Cybele and Attis*. London, UK: Thames and Hudson, 1977.

Vermes, Geza (ed.). *The Dead Sea Scrolls in English*. 1962. Harmondsworth, UK: Penguin, 1987 ed.

von Daniken, Erich. *Chariots of the Gods?: Unsolved Mysteries of the Past*. 1968. New York, NY: Bantam, 1973 ed.

———. *Gods from Outer Space: Return to the Stars, or Evidence for the Impossible*. 1968. New York, NY: Bantam, 1974 ed.

Walker, Barbara G. *The Woman's Encyclopedia of Myths and Secrets*. San Francisco, CA: Harper and Row, 1983.

———. *The Crone: Woman of Age, Wisdom, and Power*. San Francisco, CA: Harper and Row, 1985.

———. *The Woman's Dictionary of Symbols and Sacred Objects*. San Francisco, CA: Harper and Row, 1988.

Walum, Laurel Richardson. *The Dynamics of Sex and Gender: A Sociological Perspective*. Chicago, IL: Rand McNally College Publishing, 1977.

Watts, Alan. *Behold the Spirit: A Study in the Necessity of Mystical Religion*. 1947. New York, NY: Random House, 1971 ed.

Way, George, and Romilly Squire. *Scottish Clan and Family Encyclopedia*. Glasgow, Scotland: HarperCollins, 1994.

Weigall, Arthur. *The Life and Times of Akhnaton: Pharaoh of Egypt*. London, UK: W. Blackwood and Sons, 1910.

———. *Wanderings in Anglo-Saxon Britain*. New York, NY: George H. Doran, 1926.

——. *The Paganism in Our Christianity*. New York, NY: G. P. Putnam's Sons, 1928.

White, Jon Manchip. *Ancient Egypt: Its Culture and History*. 1952. New York, NY: Dover, 1970 ed.

——. *Everyday Life in Ancient Egypt*. 1963. New York, NY: Perigree, 1980 ed.

White, R. J. *The Horizon Concise History of England*. New York, NY: American Heritage, 1971.

Wilde, Lady. *Irish Cures, Mystic Charms, and Superstitions* (compiled by Sheila Anne Barry). New York, NY: Sterling Publishing, 1991.

Wilkinson, Richard H. *The Complete Temples of Ancient Egypt*. London, UK: Thames and Hudson, 2000.

——. *The Complete Gods and Goddesses of Ancient Egypt*. London, UK: Thames and Hudson, 2003.

Wind, Edgar. *Pagan Mysteries in the Renaissance*. New York, NY: W. W. Norton, 1968.

Winick, Charles. *Dictionary of Anthropology*. Totowa, NJ: Littlefield, Adams and Co., 1970.

Winks, Robin W., Crane Brinton, John B. Christopher, and Robert Lee Wolff. *A History of Civilization, Vol. 1: Prehistory to 1715*. 1955. Englewood Cliffs, NJ: Prentice Hall, 1988 ed.

Witt, Reginald Eldred. *Isis in the Ancient World*. 1971. Baltimore, MD: John Hopkins University Press, 1997.

Woolger, Jennifer Barker, and Roger J. Woolger. *The Goddess Within: A Guide to the Eternal Myths that Shape Women's Lives*. 1987. New York, NY: Fawcett Columbine, 1989.

Wright, John W. (ed.). *The Universal Almanac, 1994*. Kansas City, MO: Andrews and McMeel, 1993.

Young, Dudley. *Origins of the Sacred: The Ecstasies of Love and War*. 1991. New York, NY: Harper Perennial, 1992 ed.

Young, G. Douglas (gen. ed.). *Young's Compact Bible Dictionary*. 1984. Wheaton, IL: Tyndale House, 1989 ed.

Zaehner, R. C. (ed.) *Encyclopedia of the World's Religions*. 1959. New York, NY: Barnes and Noble, 1997 ed.

Zimmerman, J. E. *Dictionary of Classical Mythology*. New York, NY: Bantam, 1964.

Zondervan (publisher). *Zondervan Compact Bible Dictionary*. 1967. Grand Rapids, MI: Zondervan, 1993 ed.

Front view closeup of the head of the Cnidian Venus.

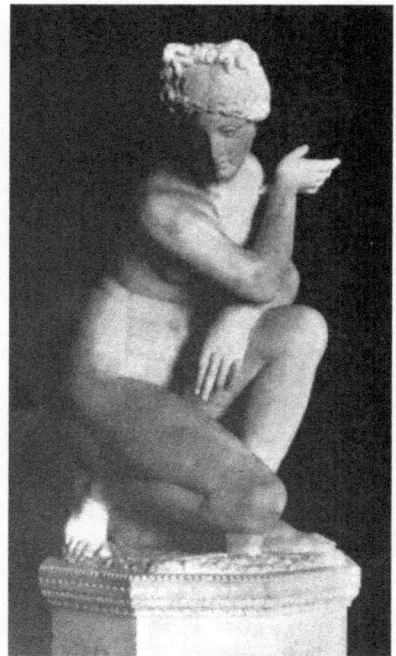
Venus crouching in the bath.

The famed Venus of Milo.

INDEX

364-day Holy Lunar Year	95
365-day Solar Year	95
A Feminist Dictionary (Kramarae)	14
A Woman's Thesaurus (Capek)	14
abductees	55
Abraham Lincoln: The Southern View (Seabrook)	143, 178
Acca Larentia	56
Achtan	56
Adad	105, 117
Adam	27, 64, 68, 146, 173, 175
Adam and Eve in Paradise	146
Adamah	64
Adath	56
Aditi	78, 88, 121, 127, 150
Adityas	78, 121
administrative script	23
administrator	28
Aeneid (Virgil)	74, 75, 91, 137, 148
Aeschylus	81
Aesop	80
Africa	2, 57, 59, 67, 88, 89, 150, 155, 166
African Fon	59
aggressive horse-back-riding people	22
agrarian village-communities	21
agriculture	28
Ahua	64
Ahura Mazda	126
Aida-Wedi	56
air	64, 79
Aisha Qandisha	56

Aka 58, 118
Akewa 56
Akka 56, 59, 118, 158
Akkadia 59, 118, 158
Akkadians 59
Ale 56
Alexander, Hartley B. 34
alien abductees 55
alien abduction 55
Allah 89
Allat 16, 56
all-female pre-Christian deity 80
all-generative divinity 19
all-powerful female figure 55
alma 71
Almighty 60, 127
almond 96
alphabet 22, 25, 149
Ama 118
Amba 118
American court system 138
American eagle 77, 79
American independence 76
Americans 2, 13, 143
Americas 67
Amma 105, 117
amniotic fluid 58
Amorites 59
Anatolia 88
Ana-Babd-Macha 46
Anchises 135
ancient art 46, 170
ancient Egyptian Virgin-Mother-Goddess 36

ancient goddes figurines	10
ancient Grecian mythographers	67
ancient Jews	59, 62, 125
ancient Latins	126
ancient Matriarchate	26
ancient Pagan tradition	96
ancient Rome	39, 59, 140, 160
Anderson	26
androcentric language	25
androcentric outlook	71
androcentric title	152
Androgyne	45, 122
angels	55, 161
Anglaend	25
Angleslænden	25
Angle's Lænden	25
Anglo-Saxon surnames	26
angular-shaped alphabet	25
anima	52, 71
animal breeding	24
Animalia	28
animus	52
Anno Domina	110, 112
Anno Domini	110, 112
Annuit Coeptis	75, 76, 137
Anthony, Mark	248
anthropologists	18, 54, 66
anthropology	183
anthropomorphic deity	76
anthropomorphic mother-deity	54
anti-woman period	123
Anu	105, 117
aphrodisiac	95

Aphrodite 47, 56, 95, 96, 103, 116, 120, 128, 137, 140
Aphrodite desexualized 96
Aphrodite of Alcamenes 140
Aphrodite's sanctuaries 120
Aphrodite's Trade (Seabrook) 126
appropriating the Goddess 87
Arabia 56, 124, 168, 179, 180
Ararat 88
archaeologists 18
archaeology 22
archetypal Father-God 105
archetypal symbols 19, 22, 121
archetypes 52, 53, 175
Argentina 56
Arianrhod 150
Aries 103
Armenia 57, 88
Artemis 8
Aruru 69
Aryans 22
As With Our Mothers, May Goddess Be With Us 37
Asase Yaa 150
Ashanti 150
Asherah 16, 56, 61, 88, 106, 120, 122, 123
Ashteroth 106
Asia 59, 67, 122, 132
Astarte 38, 106, 127, 134, 246
astrological charts 126
astrology 161, 171, 172, 181
Ataensic 88, 150
atheism 24
atheistic 82
atheists 76

Atheling, Margaret 248
Athena 6, 13
atman 64
atmen 64
atmos 64
Atse Estsan 88
Attic goddess sculpture 116
Attica, Greece 116
Attis 120, 152, 182
Australia 58, 88, 90, 150, 151
Aztec 58
Baal 66, 105, 117
Babylon 36, 118
Babylonia 36, 47, 57, 88, 89, 111, 151
Babylonian clay figurines 36
Babylonian Goddess 111
bad luck 79
bakerwoman 124
Baldwin, Matilda 248
Bandirma, Turkey 246
baptism 65, 73, 74, 84, 85, 139
baptism story of Jesus 139
Bardos 142
Bath Qol 122
Bau 118
Ba'Alat 118
beasts 67
Before the Common Era 111
Bel 36
Bellacoola 89
Bellamy, Francis 143
Beltis 36
Benedictine Order 142

beneficence 19, 49, 91, 122
Benten 32
Bernardine, Saint 127
Bhavani 88
Bible . 3, 30, 51, 60, 61, 64, 65, 67, 68, 71, 72, 93, 114, 124, 125, 129,
        149, 156, 157, 159, 162, 164-166, 168-174, 178-181, 183, 184,
        247, 249
biblical authors 124
biblical mythology 55
biblical writers . . . 43, 60, 62, 73, 81, 82, 85, 86, 90, 91, 105, 109, 112-
        115, 117, 121, 122, 133, 134, 138, 147, 149, 153
biological knowledge 20, 87
biologically hardwired 21
biopsychological complex 30
birds 3, 67, 92
birth of life 139
Birth of Venus 145
birth, death, and rebirth 19
birth, life, and death 45
bisexual 52
Blessed Virgin Mother 39, 40
blessing 37
bond(ed) 29
Bontene 118
Boston, Massachusetts 37
Boudicca, Queen, of the Iceni Tribe 248
bound 28, 29
boyfriend 66
Brahma 66, 105, 117
Brahman 66
Bran 105, 117
Brazil 57, 89
breast milk 58

breath 63, 64, 71, 139, 149, 152
breathing 64, 149, 152
breathing life 152
breath-soul 64
bride 46, 93, 172, 181
Bridget 56, 93
Brigandu 93
Brigantia 93
Bright Mother of the Hollow 69
Brigid 93, 111
Britain 76, 78, 93, 175, 182
Britannia Rules (Seabrook) 93, 177, 178
British Isles 25, 168, 175
British mythology 55
British Pagans 13
brod 72
brood 72
brotherhood of mankind 27
brute force 23
Bugan 150
bund 29
burial evidence 23
By Juno! 39
By The Grace Of Goddess 41
Caesar 135, 159
Cally Berry 88
Cambodia 89
Canaan 56, 155
canonical Bible 64
Carthage 89
Cathedral of Orvieto 245
Cathedral of Santa Maria Maggiore 120
Catholic Church 95

cave	81, 120, 172, 178
Cayuga	150
CBC	12
celestial personifications of male gods	28
Celtic Gaul	118
Celtic Goddess	111
Celtic people	57
Celtic Triple-Goddess	93
center	52, 150
centered around temple life	18
Central America	56, 58
Ceres	118
Cerridwen	88
Ceto	150
Chaldea	57, 59
Chaldeans	59
Chaos	67
Cherokee	58
chiefs	21
Child of Goddess	43
children	2, 22, 23, 26, 30, 43, 44, 65, 68, 115, 116, 123, 148, 149, 153
Children of Goddess	43, 65, 148
China	57, 131, 151
Chinook	58
Christian Holy Trinity	44
Christian iconography	96
Christian mythology	111, 127, 152, 179
Christian values	75
Christian version of Goddess	40, 111
Christian Virgin Mother-Goddess	128
Christianity	3, 14, 16, 29, 39, 44, 45, 47, 52, 54, 63, 67, 94-97, 120, 135, 150, 152, 155, 157, 162-164, 166, 169-172, 176, 178, 180,

	183, 249
Christianity, Pagan adoptions by	97
Christianization of Venus	96
christianized expression	65
Christmas Before Christianity (Seabrook)	94
church	16, 29, 47, 60, 81, 95, 96, 138, 139, 143, 155, 157, 158, 161-163, 171, 172
Church Fathers	29, 139
Church Mothers	29
Church of Jesus Christ of Latter-Day Saints	16, 172
churches	96, 120
churchyard	60
Cipactli	88
circles	22, 96
civilizations	56
clairvoyant diviners	126
Classical Greek	25
classless	18
Cnidian Venus of Praxiteles	108
Cnidian Venus, the	184, 246
Coatlicue	56, 88
cognate	26, 59, 64, 126
Columbia	46, 57, 158
Common Era	111
communal	18, 20, 23
communal food gathering	20
communication	22
Community of Israel	122
condominiums	79
Connecticut	138
conservation	28
consort-wife	39
core signs	22

core vocabulary 3, 5, 6, 11, 17
Cosmos 18, 66, 87, 131
cough 64
coughing 64
council of women 21
craftsmanship 27
Creation Legends 87, 146
creation legends, pre-biblical 146
Creation Myth 27, 64, 67, 69-71, 87
creation myths 43, 66, 68, 72, 149
Creation of Woman, the 245
creative feminine deity 72
Creator 45, 66, 77, 86, 87, 131
creator of life 45
Creator of the Universe 66, 131
Creatress 17, 43, 54, 60, 72, 86, 87, 139, 144
Creatress of the Universe and All Living Things 54
Creatrix 54, 67, 69, 87, 131
Cree 89
crescent Moon 121
crescents 22
Crone 44, 47, 80, 139, 182
Crone, Mother And Virgin Daughter 44
Crone-Goddess 47
crosses 22
Crouching Venus 107
crown of 12 stars 127
Cro-Magnon people 18
crucifixion 94
Crusade 3, 92, 177
cults 56, 182
cultures 18, 21, 55, 61, 67, 93, 126, 158
Cuna 151

curlews 92
Cybele 118, 120, 182
Cydippe 118
Cyprian Aphrodite 128
Cyprus 120, 134
D.O.M. 141
da Vinci, Leonardo 80
daggers 21, 23
Dagsdotter 26
Dahomey 89
Daly, Mary 14, 161
Damatres 118
Damkina 118
Danebod, Thyra 248
Daniel 133, 134, 172, 174
Danu 88
darkness 69, 168
daughter 44, 47, 80, 122, 139
Daughter of Zion 122
day of Devil worship 96
days of our week 27
Dea 141
Dea optimo maximo 6, 141
Deae Matres 118
Dechtere 150
Declaration of Independence 77
defensive ditches 23
deify 73, 82
Deism 75, 76
Deists 75, 76
Demeter 118
demonized Goddess 96
demonized priestesses 61

denying women their souls	40
Deo	141
Deo optimo maximo	141
depth psychologists	52
destroyer of life	45
Devi	45, 88
Devil	45
devotees of Goddess	54
Diana	3, 46, 56, 120, 132
Diana of Ephesus	132
Diana Triformis	46
Diana's shrine at Ephesus	120
Dies Veneris	94
dirt	64
Diti	150
divine act of creation	58
Divine Couple	122
Divine Feminine	13, 16, 44, 45, 80, 155, 174, 176
divine goddess	24
Divine Logos	149, 152
Divine Son	36, 45
Divine Son-God, ancient Egyptian	36
Djanggawul Sisters	150
Djigonasee	150
domestic animals	28
domina	110
doorman	27
dots	22
dove	47, 68, 139, 246, 248
down-ward pointing triangle	19
dreams	52
drone-like workers	21
Dubhehoblaigh	248

dust of the ground 71
Dyaus Pitar 23, 105
earliest creation myths 66
earliest religions 30
early human society 28
early matriarchal ancestors 21
early patriarchal Jews 64
Earth . 13, 25, 28, 43, 56, 58, 60, 65, 67-72, 79, 87, 90, 114, 121, 122,
131, 135, 152, 160, 164, 179
Earth-Mother 25, 43
East Indians 59
Easter 94, 125
eating fish on Friday 95, 96
economic power 149
Edward II 248
egalitarian 18, 21
Egypt . . . 54, 56, 69, 88, 118, 119, 149, 151, 158, 172, 173, 176, 179,
182, 183
Egyptian Virgin Mother-Goddess 112
Egyptians 59, 105
Eingana 88
Ekoi 88
El 47, 61, 105, 112, 117
El Shaddai 61
embodiment of Goddess 19
endogamic 18
England 25, 26, 46, 113, 151, 156, 179, 181, 183, 248
English . . 10, 14, 15, 17, 25, 27, 29, 59-61, 63, 71, 72, 86, 93, 94, 157,
162, 163, 166, 169, 173-177, 181, 182
English language 10, 14, 15, 17, 25, 27, 173
English scribes 61
Enlightenment 75
Enlil 105, 117, 157

entrails of animals 126
Eostre 125
Epona 118
Erda 28
erect lingam 125
Eriksdottir 26
Eriu 56, 88
Eros 69
Eskimo 89
essence of Goddess 40
Eteocypriot 25
Eternal Cosmos 18
Etruria 56
etymology 10, 60
Eurasia 122
Euripides 81, 147
Europe . 3, 22, 23, 25, 28, 59, 64, 67, 95, 96, 122, 161, 165, 169, 175,
177-179, 181, 247
European churches and cathedrals 96
Eurynome 67, 68, 151
Evangelist 104
Eve 56, 88, 118, 146
Exodus 60, 62, 113, 115, 122, 124, 138
experiencers 55
extraterrestrial beings 55
Ezekiel 123, 134, 152
Ezra 134
faceless woman 18
fairy tales 52, 61, 126, 179
families are matriarchal in character 30
family of Man 27
farewell 37, 63, 93
farm manager 28

farming 19, 28
Fates 46
father . 2, 11, 15, 16, 19, 20, 23, 25, 26, 36, 39, 43, 47, 52, 53, 55, 60, 64, 66, 75, 76, 87, 90, 105, 106, 111, 116, 117, 121, 122, 125, 129, 131, 132, 134, 139, 152, 161
Father Goth 55
fatherhood 20, 66
Father-God . . 11, 20, 36, 39, 43, 52, 60, 64, 75, 76, 87, 105, 106, 111, 117, 122, 131, 134, 152
Fear of Goddess, the 49
feast day 111
featureless face 54
February 2 111
fecundity 19, 95, 116
female . 10-12, 15-18, 20-24, 27, 38, 41, 43-45, 52-55, 61, 66, 70, 72-74, 78-80, 83, 87, 93, 95, 96, 99, 111, 112, 114, 116, 120, 124, 125, 128, 131, 138, 139, 144, 148, 152, 173, 174, 179, 246, 248
female breast 61, 79
female egg 20
female element 124
female fecundity symbol 116
female genitalia 95
female homemaker 124
female lover 124
female pelican 124
female psychology 16
female psycho-spirituality 17
female Supreme Being, Hindu 41
female symbol of love and peace 246
female trinitarian associations 45
female-based Creation Myth 87
feminine cognate 126

feminine corollary surnames 26
feminine energy system 52, 53
feminine experience 17
feminine peacefulness 139
feminine perspective 17
feminine psychology 14, 31, 169
feminine pubic triangle 19, 45
feminine soul 40
feminine spirituality 79
feminine terminology 124
feminine words 71
feminine-maternal theme 67
Feminism 12-14, 165
feminist scholars 13
feminization of Western society, the 10
fertility 55, 95, 125
fertility-Goddess 55, 125
field 17, 81
Finchoem 151
Finland 57, 119
fire, earth, air, and water 79
fireman 27
firmament 69, 70
first baseman 27
First Goddess Festival 13
first man 64
first wave of patriarchalists 23
fish 59, 95, 96, 112
fish bladder 96
fisher of men 96
fisherman 27
Fitzseward, Sibyl 248
flag shield 77

flowers	67
folk legends	126
For Goddess' Sake	49
For the Greater Glory of Goddess	49
foreman	27
forest	81
fortified villages	23
Founding Fathers	75, 76, 78, 79
four elements	79
four seasons	79
France	93
Frankish mythology	55
Franklin, Benjamin	80
free-flowing feminine-looking script	25
French	15, 95
freshman	27
Freya	94, 130
Fri	94
Friday	28, 79, 94-96, 130
Friday the Thirteenth	79, 95, 96
Frig	94, 130
Frigedæg	94
Frigg	28, 88, 94, 118, 130
Frigga	28, 88, 94, 118, 130
frigging	94
Frigg's Day	28
From Goddess and the Queen	49
Fu-Pao	151
Gaea	151
Gallipoli, Turkey	32
Gandolfsdatter	26
Ganga	88
gender-exclusive cemeteries	21, 24

Genea 3, 118, 178, 247
Genesaic Creation Myth 27
Genesis 16, 27, 61, 64, 66, 70-72, 81, 87, 126, 152, 153, 155, 166, 173
genius 40
Gerd 55, 171
German word 64, 150
Germany 58
gibbon 20
Gimbutas 22
gingerbread man 27
girls 66
global female-prominent society 18
global Goddess Religion 18
global masculinization of religion 30
global Matriarchate 24, 87
Glory Be to Goddess on High 51
Glory of Goddess, the 51
Glory of the Lady, the 51
Glory to Goddess Alone 51
Gnostic Christian 46, 57, 172
Gnosticism 76
Gnostics 54
God the Father 132, 161
Goda 55, 81
Godan 55
Godavari 55
Goddess .. 1, 3, 5, 6, 8, 10-19, 21-25, 28, 29, 31-33, 36-41, 43-49, 51-56, 58-87, 90-103, 105-107, 109-117, 119-135, 137-150, 152, 153, 155-157, 160, 162, 164-166, 175, 177, 178, 180, 183, 246, 248, 249
Goddess Almighty 60
Goddess archaeology 14

Goddess Be Praised 62
Goddess be with ye 63
Goddess Be With You 63
Goddess Bless America 63
Goddess Bless You 63, 72, 139, 152
Goddess Created the Heaven and the Earth 65
Goddess culture 12, 16, 23
Goddess Enriches 73
Goddess festival 13, 125
Goddess Forbid 75
Goddess has smiled 75, 110, 112, 137
Goddess Has Smiled On Our Accomplishments 75
Goddess Help Us 81
Goddess Help You 81
Goddess Helps Them Who Help Themselves 80
Goddess in art and literature 141
Goddess Knows! 82
Goddess Made The Country, Woman Made The Town 84
Goddess of All Things 67
Goddess of Navigation 47
Goddess of wisdom 124
Goddess Reclamation Movement 12
Goddess Religion 12, 18, 24, 29, 54, 60, 61, 80, 97
Goddess Save The King 85
Goddess Save The Queen 85
Goddess script 22
Goddess symbology 14
Goddess temple 60
Goddess The Creatress 60, 72, 86, 87
Goddess The Mother 90
Goddess vocabulary system 22
Goddess Will Grant An End Even To These (Troubles) 91
Goddess Willing 91

Goddess Wills It	92
Goddess World	21, 22, 24, 25, 53, 93
Goddess' Acre	60
Goddess' Anger	62
Goddess' Child	65
Goddess' Children	65
Goddess' Elect	73
Goddess' House	81
Goddess' Law	82
Goddess' Priestesses	85
Goddess' Righteousness	85
Goddess' Throne	90
Goddess' Truth, The	90
Goddess' Wifery	91
Goddess' Will	91
Goddess-Awful	62
Goddess-Fearing	74
Goddess-Mother	84
Goddess-Send	86
Goddess-Sent	86
Goddesschild	65, 86
Goddessdamn	72
Goddessdamned	72
Goddessdaughter	73
Goddessed	73
Goddesses	16, 40, 53, 55, 56, 61, 74, 105, 106, 109, 111, 115, 117, 119, 120, 126, 137, 155, 160, 165, 169, 172, 174, 176, 183
Goddesses Will Find A Way, The	74
Goddesses Willed Otherwise, The	74
Goddessfather	74
Goddessforsaken	75
Goddesshead	47, 80
Goddesshood	81

Goddessing 82
Goddessless 82
Goddesslessness 82
Goddesslier 83
Goddessliest 83
Goddesslike 83
Goddesslikeness 83
Goddessliness 84
Goddessling 83
Goddessly 84, 144
Goddessparent 84
Goddessson 86
Goddessspeed 86
Goddesswit 92
Goddess' ancient thirteen-month Lunar Calender 29
Goddess' children 43, 44, 65
Goddess' holy emblem 29
Goddess' house 81
Goddess' priestesses 85
Goddess' pubic triangle 44, 125
Goddess' regenerative energy 22
Goddess' Temples 123
Goddess' wifery 91
Goddess' will 91
Goddess' wrathful side 62
goddess-mother 84
Goddess-worshipers . 23, 37, 39, 41, 43, 44, 49, 51, 52, 60, 62, 63, 65,
        73-75, 80-87, 90-94, 97-103, 106, 109-115, 117, 120-122, 129,
                131-135, 137, 138, 140-145, 147, 148, 153, 248
Goddess-worshiping Jews 124
Goddess-worshiping nation 93
Goddess-worshiping religions 44
Godiva, Lady (Goddess) 248

gods . 21, 23, 28, 31, 61, 69, 74, 80, 115, 120, 126, 152, 155-157, 159, 161, 163, 165-167, 169, 171, 172, 176, 179, 182, 183
God-based vocabulary 16
God-based wording 11
God-centered religions 60
god-mother 69
Good Goddess 103
Gooddess 92
Gooddess Book, The 93
Gooddess Faith 93
Gooddess Friday 94
Gooddess Goddess! 97
Gooddess Life, The 98
Gooddess-Bye 93
Gooddess-Fellow 94
Gooddess-Fellowship 94
Gooddess-Hearted 97
Gooddess-Heartedly 97
Gooddess-Heartedness 97
Gooddess-Humored 98
Gooddess-Humoredly 98
Gooddess-Humoredness 98
Gooddess-Looker 99
Gooddess-Looking 99
Gooddess-Natured 100
Gooddess-Naturedly 100
Gooddess-Naturedness 100
Gooddess-Neighbor 101
Gooddess-Tempered 101
Gooddess-Temperedly 101
Gooddess-Temperedness 102
Gooddess-Wife 102
Gooddessie 102

Gooddessish	92
Gooddesslady	99
Gooddesslier	99
Gooddessliest	100
Gooddessly	99
Gooddessman	100
Gooddessness	101
Gooddesswill	102
Gooddesswilled	102
Gooddessy	103
good-bye	63
Gothic mythology	55
government	76
grandmother	46, 139, 248
grass	67, 70
grave goods	24
great apes	20
great clan mother	18
Great Creatrix	54, 87
Great Creatrix of Life	54
Great Earth-Mother	25
great Father-God, Babylonian	36
Great Life-Giving Mother	61
great maternal figure	20
Great Mother	11, 17, 19, 30, 36, 41, 55, 58, 85, 106, 114, 120, 125, 131, 133, 142, 149, 153, 174
great Mother-Goddess	36
Great Mother-Goddess	36, 41, 55, 106, 120
great seal of the U.S.A.	75, 137
great serpent	68
Great Sex-Goddess	95
Great Sky-Father	25
Great Yantra	45

Greece . 6, 23, 24, 39, 46, 47, 56, 88, 89, 118, 119, 149-151, 159, 164
Greek Goddess . 6, 111
Greek Olympian cosmology . 67
Greek Temple . 13
Greek word . 64, 150
guardians . 21, 55
gylanic council . 23
Gyn/Ecology (Daly) . 14
gynocentric belief system . 123
gynocentric dialect . 17
gynocratic . 18
Haiti . 56
halberds . 22
Haltia . 56
Har Elohim . 62
hara . 125
Hariti . 126
Haru-spices . 126
Hasidic Ashkenazim . 124
Heavenly Mother . 16, 39, 41, 60, 90, 105, 106, 121, 134
Heavens Bespeak The Glory of Goddess, The . 106
Hebe-Hera-Hecate . 46
Hebrew . 61, 62, 68, 71, 72, 120, 122, 123, 125, 164, 166, 175
Hebrew Goddess . 71, 120, 122, 175
Hebrew Pantheon . 123
Hecate . 46, 120, 149
Helios-Selene-Aphrodite . 47
Henwen . 151
her Church . 60
Hera . 46, 88, 118, 151
Herbert, George . 81
herbs . 68
hexagram . 44, 45, 77, 79, 125

Hieros Logos 63
higher primate species 20
Higher Self 52
highly mobile pastoral lifestyle 23
hill forts 21
hilltop fortresses 23
Hina 88
Hindu female Supreme Being 41
Hindu Mother-Goddess 121
Hindu mythology 45, 55
Hindus 45
history . 2, 3, 6, 10, 12, 25, 46, 105, 155-160, 162-164, 166, 167, 169, 170, 172, 175-179, 181-183, 247
Hittite 57, 158
Hokhma 124
holy breath 152
holy days 95
Holy Ghost 44, 47, 139
holy healer 148
Holy Spirit 47, 122, 139
Holy Yoni 125
Homer 68
hominids 44
Homo sapiens 21, 28
Homo sapiens sapiens 28
Honest To Goddess 106
Hopi 57
Hora 115, 125, 126
Horace 115
Horae 126
Horites 126
horoscope 126
horsemanship 27

Horus	36
Hosea	123, 124
hotels	79
hour	15, 126
Howsoever It Shall Please Goddess	106
human	12, 18-20, 22, 23, 25, 27, 28, 30, 31, 43, 45, 46, 54, 56, 70, 76, 79, 126, 131, 158, 171
human beings	70
human female	27, 131
human infant	79
human language	25
human prehistory	56
human society	18, 25, 28, 131
humanistic maxim	84
human-on-human violence	23
Hungary	58, 89
hunters	21
husband	28, 66, 123
husbandman	28
husbandry	91
I Am The Lady Your Goddess	109
I The Lady Your Goddess Am Holy	112
Iason	105
Ibibio	88
Icenians	248
Iesous	105
Ieu	105
If Goddess Wills It	109
If It Pleases The Goddesses	109
Ila	88
Illuminati	80
Imd	56
Immaculate Conception, the	128

In Goddess We Trust 109
In The Name Of Goddess 110
In The Year Of Our Lady 110
inanimate objects 72
Inanna 88
incubate 72
India . . . 46, 57, 59, 78, 88, 89, 105, 118, 119, 121, 126, 149-151, 155, 180, 181
Indian father-god 105
Indian Goddess 78, 150
Indian Mountain-Mother-Goddess 126
Indian sacred art 121
Indonesia 57
Indo-European 25, 28, 59, 64
Indo-European family of languages 64
Indo-European Mother-Earth-Goddess 28
Indo-European speakers 25
Indo-European word 64
insemination 20
insufflation 139, 149
Iran 59
Ireland 3, 23, 46, 56, 88, 93, 149-151, 172, 175-177, 248
Iroquois 88, 150
Isabella the Fair 248
Isaiah 71, 86, 123, 124
Ishtar 47, 88, 106, 120, 153
Isis 36, 47, 56, 88, 106, 112, 120, 164, 176, 183
Islam 16, 155, 168
Islam's symbol 29
Isong 88
Israel 47, 78, 112, 122
Istar 153
Italian 95, 96

Italy	56, 89, 118, 119
Iu-Pater	105
Ixtab	56
Izanami	88
Jahi	105
January 1	111
Japan	58, 88, 161
Japanese Goddess of Divine Love	32
Jason	105
Jefferson, Thomas	75, 77, 138
Jeffersonianism	138
Jehovah	47, 75, 76, 87, 105, 117, 124, 134, 152
Jeremiah	106, 123, 133
Jesus	3, 16, 47, 78, 94, 96, 104, 105, 110-112, 115, 117, 124, 127, 133, 139, 142, 152, 155, 156, 161, 164, 165, 171-173, 178, 181, 249
jewelry	24
Jewish mystics	45, 78, 125
Jewish Queens	124
Jewish-Christian mystics	121
Jews	59, 61, 62, 64, 65, 105, 123-125, 163
jinn	40
John the Baptist	115
John the Evangelist	76
Johnson, Andrew	75
Joshua	105, 122, 123, 147
Jovis Pater	39
Judaism	16, 29, 39, 44, 54, 56, 67, 71, 88, 122-126, 155, 177
Judaism's deep roots in Goddess-worship	125
Judeo-Christian Creation myth	69, 71
Judeo-Christian Father-God	64, 76, 87
Judeo-Christian holy book	51, 65, 93, 114, 129
Judeo-Christian mythology	127, 152

Judeo-Christian Patriarchal Takeover of Goddess	93
Judeo-Christian-Islamic heritage	29
Judges	123, 147
June	6, 39, 169
Juno	39, 40, 46, 106, 111, 120, 137
Juno's attributes	40
Juno's sacred month	39
Jupiter	28, 39, 40, 66, 105, 117, 137, 152
Juventas-Juno-Minerva, or Uni	46
Kabbalistic tradition	45
Kabbalists	125
Kadru	88
Kali	57, 59, 88, 149
Kali Ma	59
Kelle	3, 57, 149, 177, 249
Kelts	57
Khon-Ma	89
King Arthur	112
King James	61, 71, 181
King James version	71, 181
King of Heaven	133
Kingdom	3, 16, 133, 177, 178, 249
kingdom of God	16, 133
kings	21, 51, 62, 120, 123, 124, 134
Koevasi	89
Kongsim	151
Koran	170
Kore	57, 120, 151
Korea	57, 151
Kottavi	89
Kuma	89
Kupalo	57
Kurgan men	24

Kurgan tribes 24
Kurgans 23
kylix 50
Lady Goddess 113, 142
Lady Goddess Of Their Mothers, The 113
Lady Godiva 55
Lady Have Mercy 114
Lady Is My Light, The 113
Lady Marri 59
lady of heaven 69, 121
Lady Our Goddess, The 115
Lady Thy Goddess Is A Jealous Goddess, The 115
Lady, Direct Us 113
Lady's Prayer, The 114
lakes 67, 170, 176
Lakshmi 41
Lamb of Goddess 115
language 9, 10, 14-17, 22, 25, 27-29, 149, 159, 170, 173
Late Neolithic 131
Latin 25, 39, 40, 59, 71, 75, 76, 105, 110, 137, 141, 181
Latin-speaking Christians 105
Latium 46, 59
laurel branch 77
Lawrence, D. H. 8
layman 27
LDS 16
leaden goddess idol 246
Leave The Rest To The Goddesses 115
life . 3, 11, 18-21, 23, 24, 30, 44, 45, 54, 58, 61, 63, 66, 67, 69, 72, 87,
        91, 95, 96, 98, 124, 125, 131, 139, 144, 149, 150, 152, 160,
                        165, 174, 175, 179, 182, 183, 247
lifelong monogamous unions 21
life-giving mother 61, 124

life-giving pubic-triangle 54
life-giving vulva 61, 125
light 55, 69, 113, 164, 173
light-Goddess 55
Ligoapup 151
Lilwani 57
Limosa 92
Lincoln, Abraham 75, 143
linguistic imposition 25
Lithuania 57
living creatures 68, 70
living primates 20
Lla-Mo 89
Logos 63, 72, 149, 150, 152
London, England 113
long-billed wading birds 92
Lord God 113, 142
Lord is my light 113
Lord's Prayer 114
Lorop 57
Louhi 57
love-deity 94
Luhya 89
Luminu-Ut 151
lump of clay 152
lunar crescent 19, 23, 29, 38, 127, 128
lunar form 28
Lunar Year 78, 95, 122
Luna-Diana-Proserpine 46
Ma 119
ma, root-word 59
Maat 149
Mac, meaning of 26

MacDonald 26
Maerin 59
magic procreative powers 19
magical circle dances 126
Magna Dea 11
Magna Mater's sacred cave-shrine 120
Maia 59, 111, 120
Maid Marian 59
Malaysia 58
male burials 24
male consort 55, 122
male deities 15, 27, 53, 55
male deity 15, 19, 23, 52, 53, 87, 131
male guardians 55
Male Principle 45, 125
male servants 55
male warrior-chieftain 24
male-dominant American society 10
male-based religions 17
male-dominant culture 13, 15
male-dominant Germanic people 25
male-dominant vocabulary 11
male-dominated gender-inclusive cemeteries 24
male-exclusive trinities 47
male-oriented language 29
male-oriented substructure 26
male-oriented words 25
male-saturated 29
male-slanted speech 17
Mami 118
mammalian species 66
mammals 3, 27
mammary-like mountains 126

Man ... 15, 27-29, 40, 45, 57, 64, 66, 74, 84, 124, 146, 148, 169, 175, 179, 183, 247

Man upstairs ... 29
manacle ... 15
manage ... 15
management ... 15
manager ... 15, 28
mandate ... 15
mandatory ... 15
Mandorla ... 96, 104
mandrake ... 15
maneuver ... 15
manhandle ... 15
manhole ... 15
manhunt ... 15
manifest ... 15, 53
manifests ... 46
manikin ... 15
manipulate ... 15
manpack ... 15
manpower ... 15
manslaughter ... 15
mantel ... 15
mantra ... 15, 149
mantrap ... 15
manual ... 15
manufacture ... 15
manuscript ... 15, 178, 179
man-day ... 15
man-eater ... 15
man-hour ... 15
man-made ... 15
man-of-war ... 15

man's psyche	52
man-servant	28
man-size	15
man-to-man	15
man-year	15
Map, meaning of	26
Mar	119
mar, root-word	59
Marah	59
March 1	111
Marcus Terentius Varro	84
mare	59
Mare Nostrum	59
Mari	29, 46, 119
Maria	59, 119
Mariam	119
Marian	59, 119
Mariana	59
Marica	59
Marie	119, 161, 247
Mariham	59
marina	59, 171
maris	59, 97
maritimus	59
Marratu	59
marriage and the family	39
marrying in June	39
Mars	28, 39, 120
Martu	105, 117
Mary	14, 16, 36, 40, 42, 46, 57, 59, 96, 97, 104, 106, 111, 118-121, 127, 128, 137, 151, 159, 161, 167, 171, 172, 176, 179
Mary, the Virgin	36, 42, 96, 97, 104, 106, 119, 128
Marzanna	59

masculine energy system 52, 53
masculine father-figure 15
masculine triangle 45
masculinization process 25
Masonic Deists 76
Masons 75, 80
Matergabiae 57
maternal birthplace 126
maternal figure-head 53
maternal instinct 66, 67
maternal life-bearing mother 61
maternal love 19
maternal role models 66
maternal-figure 30, 53, 54
Matheson 26
Matriarch . 9, 10, 18, 21, 24, 26, 30, 37, 39, 41, 43, 44, 49, 51-53, 60,
    62, 63, 65, 66, 71-75, 80-87, 90-94, 96-103, 105, 106, 109, 110,
    112-117, 121, 122, 124, 129, 131-135, 137, 138, 140-142, 144,
    145, 147-149, 153, 158, 248
matriarchal 9, 18, 21, 30, 37, 39, 41, 43, 44, 49, 51, 52, 60, 62, 63, 65,
    66, 71-75, 80-87, 90-94, 96-103, 105, 106, 109, 110, 112-117,
    121, 122, 124, 129, 131-135, 137, 138, 140-142, 144, 145, 147-
    149, 153, 158, 248
matriarchal Judaism 71
matriarchal origins 96
Matriarchate 18, 24, 26, 53, 60, 87
matriarchy 10, 79, 87
matricentric 3, 13, 18, 30, 44, 54, 81, 177
matricentric religion 54
matricentric species 30
matrifocal 17, 18, 122
matrifocal belief system 122
matrifocal words 17

matrilineal 18
matrilocal 18
matronymicism 26, 150
matronymics 26
Mawu 57, 59, 89
May 1 111
May Day 111
May Goddess Have Mercy 117
Maya 56, 59, 120
Mead, Margaret 66
meanders 22
Mediterranean Sea 59
Melanesia 89
menses 95
menstrual blood 58
menstrual cycle 19, 78, 95
Mer 59, 119
Mercia, England 248
Mercury 28
Meri 59, 119
mermaid 59
Mesolithic 44
Mesopotamians 69
Meter 118
metronymy 150
Mexico 46, 56, 88
Micronesia 57, 151
Middle East 67, 171, 179
Middle Paleolithic Era 18
midwife 124
milkman 27
milk-giving breasts 61
milk-spewing breasts 125

Minahassa	151
Minoan hieroglyphs	25
minor female deities	74
misogynistic force	25
misogynistic men	40
misogynistic priests	11
mistranslated	61
mistress	29, 102
mod	71
modor	71
modorhrif	71
modorlic	71
Mohawk	151
Mokosh	89
molded clump of dirt	64
Monday	28
Mongolia	58
monotheistic religions	15, 53, 76
Mons Veneris	61, 127
month	29, 39, 78, 79, 120, 122, 124
Moon	3, 8, 19, 68, 79, 95, 121, 123, 132, 133, 155, 167
Moon-Goddess	3, 132, 133
Moon's Day	28
Mormons	16, 54
Morocco	56
Mother	117
mother and her offspring	20
mother as the primary parent	30
mother bear	124
Mother City	122
mother eagle	124
mother hen	124
Mother in Heaven	16

Mother of all humanity	39
mother of all sound	150
Mother of Life	19
Mother of the Gods	31
Mother Which Is In Heaven, Your	121
Mother, Lady Of Heaven And Earth	121
motherhood	66
mother-child matrix	20
mother-child relationship	43
Mother-Nature	66
motif	105, 150
motto of Arizona	73
motto of Connecticut	138
motto of England's Oxford University	113
motto of London, England	113
motto of the Benedictine Order	142
motto of the Society of Jesus	142
Mount of God	62, 122
Mount Of Goddess, The	122
mountain	61, 62, 125, 126
mountains	61, 67, 68, 126
Mountain-Mother	61, 126
mouth	64
Mu Olokukurtilisop	151
Muk Jauk	89
Museum of Bardos	142
Mut	118
mysticism, Christian	76
mystics	45, 78, 121, 125, 135
myth	2, 15, 27, 55, 61, 64, 67, 69-71, 87, 155-157, 159, 160, 162, 164, 166-168, 171, 172, 180
mythographers	67, 68, 87, 123
mythology	10, 14, 24, 45, 52, 55, 78, 111, 127, 152, 157-160, 163,

                    164, 166-172, 175-177, 179, 180, 182, 184
myths ...   36, 43, 55, 66, 68, 72, 87, 95, 109, 119, 126, 131, 149, 150,
        152, 156, 157, 159, 161-163, 165, 166, 170, 175, 179, 181-183
M's 22
nabalo 150
named after their mother 26
Nana 120, 151
Nanshe 111
Nashville, Tennessee 5, 6, 13
natural head of the family 67
natural laws 76
Navaho 58, 88, 90, 119
Near East 122, 123, 133, 157, 182
Near Eastern Creation Myth 70
Near Eastern Pagan Mother-Goddess 119
Nehemiah 82, 147
Neith 151
Nemesis 89
Neolithic 18, 19, 22, 44, 59, 131, 169
Neolithic peoples 19
Neptune 28
Nessa 151
neurosis 53
never-ending cycle 19
new androcentric religions 87
new Moon 123
new patriarchal society 23
New Testament patriarchalists 246
New York City 13
Nicnevin 57
Nigeria 56, 118
Night 68, 70
nine tail feathers 79

nine-month gestation period 79
nine-pointed hexagram 79
Ninsar 57
nomadic warrior lifestyle 24
non-Hasidic Orthodox Judaism 124
Norns 46
Norse legend 55
North America 3, 57, 58, 88-90, 119, 150, 151
North Star 97
north wind 68
Norway 57
Norwegian word 92
Nubia 118
nuclear family 20, 66, 116
nursing mother 61, 124
nurturing of life 139
nymph relief 32
Nyx 151
Obatallah 89
obsession with Goddess veneration 19
occult arts 79
ocean 59
Oceania 67, 151
oceanic love 58
Oceanus 68
Ocrisia 118
October 21 111
Oddudua 118
Odes 115
Odin 47, 55, 105, 117
Odin-Tyr-Frey 47
of the sea 97
Oglala 90

Ognyene Maria	57
Oh My Goddess!	129
Old English	59, 71, 72, 94
Old Europeans	23, 25
Old High German word	150
Old Testament	61, 75, 117, 123, 124, 146, 160, 165, 168
Old Testament patriarchalists	246
Om	150
Omamama	89
omnipotence of Juno	40
omnipotent	148
om-phalos	150
Oneida	151
one-dollar bill	75, 77, 79, 80, 137
Onondaga	150
Ophion	68
Ops	118
orgiastic rituals	123
Oriental Jews	124
Original Sin	176
Orore	57
Orphics	68
orthodox Christian Fathers	40
orthodox Christians	54, 59, 95, 105, 106
orthodox Jewish authorities	45
orthodox patriarchal Christianity	94
Orvieto, Italy	245
Oshun	57
Osiris	47, 105, 117, 158
Osiris-Isis-Horus	47
Our Lady	17, 110, 112
Our Mother Which Art In Heaven	129
ovals	22

O's	22
Pagan converts	95
Pagan custom	124
Pagan female symbol	128
Pagan feminine origins	61
Pagan Goddess	97, 127
Pagan Goddesses	119, 120
Pagan origins	64
Pagan Romans	39
Pagan Virgin-Goddess	139
Paganism	16, 95, 161, 183
pagoda	81
Paine, Thomas	76
Paive	57
Paleolithic	18, 21, 22, 44, 55
Paleolithic representations of men	21
palisades	21
Panama	151
Panderma	246
Pandora	119
Pao-Yueh	57
Papa	119, 162
paradise	146
parthenogenesis	151
parthenogenic Mother-Goddess	150
parthenogenic reproductive power	122
Parthenon	13
Parvati	46, 119, 151
Parvati-Durga-Uma	46
paternal figure	20
paternity	20, 24, 66, 87, 149
patriarchal conceit	27
patriarchal Hebrew scribes	71

patriarchal Jewish priests 70
patriarchal Jewish scribes 123
patriarchal Latin 75
patriarchal monotheistic religions 76
patriarchal nuclear family 116
patriarchal phraseology 15
Patriarchal Takeover . 10, 11, 26, 28, 40, 43, 46, 53, 55, 78, 79, 87, 93, 116, 122, 123, 131, 151
patriarchalists 14, 23, 43, 60, 246
Patriarchate 13, 14, 24, 60, 73, 109, 121, 152, 153
Patriarchy . 25, 60, 62, 66, 81, 82, 85, 86, 90, 91, 93, 96, 106, 112-115, 121, 122, 133, 134, 138, 147, 149, 152, 171
Patriarchy's Creation Myth 87
Patriarchy's paternal-god 117
patricentric Indo-Europeans 23
patricized 25, 122
patronymicism 26
Paul, Saint 132
Pawnee 58, 89, 119
pedestal 146
Pelasgians 67
pencil 136
pendulous breasts 18, 54
Persian Sun-God 126
Persians 59
Peru 119
phallic symbol 23
phallocentric language 29
phallus symbol 19
Phanes 69, 175
Pheraia 89
Philae 120
Philippines 150

Phoenicia 57, 118
Phrygia 118, 151, 152
Phrygian Sun-God 152
physical strength 23
pine cones 38
planets 28, 68
Playing Goddess 131
pledge 138, 140, 143, 144
Pledge of Allegiance 143, 144
Pluto 28
pneuma 71
Po Ino Nogar 89
Poland 58, 90
policeman 27
politics 24, 247
polygamous pre-marriage culture 21
Polynesia 64, 88, 119, 151
Polynesian Creation Myth 64
Polynesians 64
polytheistic Pagan ways 123
polytheistic religions 53
Pompeii, Italy 36
powerful warrior-class 23
Poza-Mama 151
Praise Be To Goddess 132
Praise Goddess 131
prayer of solicitation 63
predators 20
pregnant abdomen 18, 54, 61, 125
pregnant bellies 149
prehistoric art 21, 53
prehistoric cultures 21
prehistoric Pagan Goddess religion 96

prehistoric religions 139
prepatriachal Hebrew Goddess Creation myth 71
prepatriarchal Hindu female deity 55
prepatriarchal Jews 61
prepatriarchal myths 131
preserver of life 45
pre-biblical creation myths 149
pre-biblical creation story 67
pre-biblical legend 67
pre-Christian Egypt 149
pre-Christian Father-God 39
pre-Christian Greece 149
pre-Christian Greek Pagans 63
pre-Christian India 149
pre-Christian Pagan mystics 135
pre-Christian savior-christ 152
priests 11, 45, 70, 87
Primal Androgyne 45
primate males 20
primate species 20
primatologists 20, 66
primeval time 69
primordial female deity 18
Primordial Logos 150
princes 21
procreation 43, 151
procreation-by-way-of-magic words 152
procreative Logos 149
prosperity 19
Proverbs 124
Psalms 61, 106, 117, 124, 153
psyche 52, 53, 71
psychic archetype 61

psychic void 31
psycho-spiritual wound 60
pubic triangle symbol 23
pyramid 77, 79, 181
Qamaits 89
Qocha Mana 57
Queen of Heaven 17, 39-42, 106, 120, 133, 134
Queen Of Queens 134
queen of the gods 69
Queen of the South 133
Queendom 114, 133
Queendom Of Goddess, The 133
queen-priestess 18
Ra 66, 105, 117
rabbit 116
rachaph 72
Rachel 57
rain 67
Real Self 52, 53
religion . . . 10, 12, 14-18, 24, 29, 30, 44, 54, 60, 61, 76, 77, 80, 87, 97,
    123, 156, 157, 160, 161, 163-165, 169, 171, 175, 177, 179, 182,
    247
religion transforming 123
religions . . . 14, 15, 17, 30, 44, 53, 55, 60, 76, 87, 122, 124, 139, 148,
    150, 155, 157, 161, 162, 165, 166, 168, 180, 184
religious ceremonies 52, 72, 110
religious services 49
Render Unto Caesar The Things That Are Caesar's 135
Renenet 119
renewal of life 19
reproductive role 61
resurrection 46, 158
Revelation 3, 38, 78, 79, 121, 134, 152, 153

Rhea 23, 89
Ri 57
rigidly ranked hierarchy 23
rivers 67, 68, 156, 165
river-Goddess 55
Roman father-god 105
Roman Goddess 32, 111
Roman Goddess of Divine Love 32
Roman Moon-Goddess 132
Roman scholar 84
Roman Sex-Goddess 28
Roman woman 39
Romans 39, 73, 85, 87, 93, 94, 127, 152, 161
Rome 39, 40, 59, 108, 120, 140, 160, 167, 248
Rome, Italy 108, 140
Roosevelt, Theodore 76
rudimentary father-figure 19
Russia 22, 25, 57
ruwach 71
sacred animal 139
sacred bird of peace 47
sacred breath 149
sacred hieroglyph 22
sacred Jewish writings 123
sacred numbers 79, 95
sacred personification 18
sacred prostitute 148, 176
sacred sound 150
sacred utterances 152
sacred womb 96
safety 19
Saint Bridget 93
salutation 37, 51, 62, 85, 131, 142

Sanskrit	39, 105, 125
Santeria	58, 119
Sarah	89
Sarasvati	89
Saris	57
Satine	57
Saturday	28
Saturn	28, 105, 117
Saturn's Day	28
Saudi Arabia	124
Savior	39, 78, 120, 121, 152
Savior-Son-God	39
Saxon Fertility-Goddess	125
Saxons	59
Scandinavia	26, 28, 47, 55, 56, 59, 88, 94, 118, 130, 161, 163
Scandinavian countries	26
Scandinavian Love-Goddess	28
Scandinavian Mother-Goddess	130
Scandinavian mythology	55
Scandinavian Sex-Goddess	94
scholars	13, 17, 110
science	24, 58, 126, 247
Scotia	57
Scotland	57, 93, 162, 166, 180, 182, 248
Scottish culture	26
Scythia	89
sea	59
Seabrook, Lochlainn	11, 31, 247-249
Seabrook's Complete Encyclopedia of Deities (Seabrook)	178
Seal of Solomon	44
seasons	70, 79
seawater	58, 59
secret symbol	45

sectarian	22
secular	14, 22, 23, 142
secular purposes	23
secular words	14
Sedna	89
Sela	89
Selci Syt Emysyt	119
self-fertilizing deities	20
self-fertilizing virgins	149
seminal	26
seminar	26
Semitic first man and woman	146
Semitic love-goddess	38
Semitic mountain-goddess	61
Semitic tribe	126
Semitic Virgin-Mother-Goddess	29
Seneca	150
sensual pleasure	54
separation of church and state	138
Sephardim	124
September 8	111
Serbia	57
settled agrarian life	23
settled agriculturists	21
seven-day weeks	95
sex worship	45
sexual companions	21
sexual intercourse	149
Sexual Mysteries	126
sexual opposites	45
sexual relationships	20
sexual-spiritual union	45
shaddai	61

Shakers	16
Shamash-Sin-Ishtar	47
She (Goddess) Has Favored Our Undertaking	137
She (Goddess) Who Transplanted Sustains	138
Sheela Na Gig	96
Shekhina	122
shelf-like buttocks	18, 54
shield	136
Shiwanokia	89, 151
shrines	13, 120
Sia	119
Siberia	90, 119, 151
Sibilaneuman	57
Sidonian coins	47
silver egg	68
single elite ruling family	23
Sinjang Halmoni	57
Sisterhood	87
skepticism	24
sky	23, 25, 43, 68
Sky-God	23
Slavic Goddess	111
Slavonia	58, 89
Slavs	59
sneeze	64
snipes	92
snowman	27
snow-capped mountain	61
So Help You Goddess	138
social gatherings	49
social hierarchy	22
socialism	143
socialization	66

Society of Jesuits	49
Society of Jesus	142
sociologists	66
solar sign	23
solar system	28
solar-deity	78
Solomon's Seal	125
Song of Solomon	124
Son-God	36, 39, 134, 152
Sophia	57
Sophocles	81
soul	40, 63, 64, 71, 171
souls	40, 150, 177
source of life	19
spark of life	45
spears	21
spirit	3, 40, 47, 65, 69, 71, 102, 122, 138, 139, 164, 182
spirit of God	71, 138
spirit of Goddess	47, 65, 69, 138
spiritual rebirth	24
spiritual sex	45
spiritual-sexual union	125
spoken word	63
sportsmanship	27
Sri Yantra	45
Srinmo	58
Star of David	44, 125
Star of the Sea	97
stars	68, 70, 77, 78, 87, 121, 127, 182
star-burst	77, 79
statuettes of Goddess	18
Stella Maris	97
stone ramparts	21

subterfuge 71
Sumeria 22, 57, 88, 118, 157
Sumerian script 22
sun 36, 68, 69, 78, 79, 94, 95, 110, 121, 126, 152, 164, 165
Sun-God, ancient Egyptian 36
Sunday 27
Sundi-Mumi 119
Sun-God 36, 78, 94, 110, 126, 152
Sun's Day 27
superstition 65
Supreme Being . . . 15-17, 39, 41, 49, 51, 52, 54, 62, 64, 72, 73, 78, 81,
              87, 91, 111, 113, 115, 117, 129, 132, 141, 144, 147-149
supreme syllable 150
swan 50
swastika 246
swastika, traditional female energy symbol 246
swastikas 22, 246
Swear To Goddess 140
swirls 22
swollen life-giving vulva 125
swollen triangular vulva 19
symbolic emblem 19
symbolism 23, 61, 80, 157, 163, 164
synagogue 29, 81
Syrians 59
Tabiti 89
Tai Yuan 151
Talmud 65
Tanith 89
Tantric Hinduism 125
Tantrism 45
teenagers 96
Teleglen Edzen 58

Tellus Mater 119
Tem 69
temple 13, 18, 19, 29, 60, 81, 120, 125, 126, 148
temple priestess 125, 148
termination of life 139
testament 26
testicle 29
testify 26
testimony 26, 87
Tethys 68, 89
Thalassa 151
Thank Goddess! 141
Thanks Be To Goddess 141
The Book of Kelle (Seabrook) 57, 177
The Civilization of the Goddess (Gimbutas) 13
The Complete Dictionary of Christian Mythology (Seabrook) 179
the deep 69, 71, 72
The Divine Feminine (Mollenkott) 13
The Elements of Nonsexist Usage (Dumond) 14
The Goddess Dictionary of Words and Phrases (Seabrook) ... 10, 14, 17
the Lady 36
the Law 3, 178, 249
The One 79, 137
the Son 139
The Unauthorized Encyclopedia of the Bible (Seabrook) 179
The Way of Holiness (Seabrook) 178
The White Goddess (Graves) 13
theacratic 18
thealogy 16, 17
theists 76
theologians 17
theology 14, 16, 170
theriomorphic sculptures 19

Thetis 89
thick trunk-like thighs 19, 54
thirteen 18, 21, 29, 77-79, 95, 122, 124
thirteen arrows 77
thirteen colonies 77
thirteen different levels 77
thirteen leaves 77
thirteen months 78, 95
thirteen stars 77
thirteen stripes 77
thirteenth floor 79
thirteen-member all-female collegia 21
thirteen-month Lunar Calender 29, 124
thirteen-month Lunar Year 78, 122
Thor's Day 28
Three Damosels 46
Three Divine Sisters 46
Three Marys 46
three-lobed lily 40
throne 41, 90
Thursday 27
Tiamat 89, 151
Tiberius, Octavia Major 248
Tibet 58, 89
Tiki-Ahua 64
Tiw's Day 27
To Goddess, The Best, The Greatest 141
To The Greater Glory Of Goddess 142
To The Lady Goddess, Supreme Ruler Of The World 142
toast 37, 49, 51, 52, 85, 142
toast at feasts 49
totemic animals 95
traditional female fish symbol 112

traditional female symbols	38
trees	67, 68
triadic deity	139
triadic entity	45
triadic form	46
triangle	38
triangles	22, 44, 125
trinitarian functions	19
Triple-Goddess	45, 46, 93, 139
Triple-Goddess Mary	46
triplicate functions	45
true nuclear family	20
Tuesday	27
Tundr Ilona	89
Turkey	32, 56, 118, 246
Tuscarora	151
tutelary deity	40
Twelve Apostles of Jesus	78, 112
Twelve Disciples of Buddha	78, 112
Twelve female Disciples	78
Twelve Knights	112
Twelve Knights of King Arthur	78
Twelve Labors of Hercules	78
Twelve Paladins of Roland	78
twelve savior-sons	121
Twelve stars	78, 121
Twelve Star-God Savior-Sons	78
Twelve Sun-signs	78
Twelve Tribes of Israel	78
Twelves Tribes of Isis-Ra-El	112
twelve-month Solar Year	78
twenty-eight days	78, 95
twenty-eight-day lunations	19

two-parent monogamous family unit 20
U.S. Congress 143
U.S.A. 75-77, 109, 137, 143
ufologists 55
Ultimate Reality 52
Under Goddess 22, 143, 144
underworld 69
Unelanuhi 58
Ungoddessliness 144
Ungoddessly 144
uni 39, 46
United States Flag Association 143
United States of America 3, 63, 144
Universal Creatress 17
universal deity 11
Universal Egg 68
universal Father-God 105, 117
universal feminine Creatress 87
Universal Great Mother-Goddess 41
universal title 105
Universe 39, 54, 66, 69, 76, 87, 96, 131, 139, 152
Uranus 28, 67
Ursala 111
Uti Hiata 58, 89, 119
Utset 58, 119
Vac 150
vagina 39, 96
Varro, Marcus Terentius 84
Vatican 132
Vatican Museum 108
Vendredi 95
Venerdì 95
Venezuela 89

Venus ... 18, 28, 32, 36, 48, 50, 94, 96, 107, 108, 127, 129, 135, 136, 140, 142, 145, 160, 184, 185, 246, 248
Venus desexualized 96
Venus figurines 129
Venus Genetrix 140
Venus head, the 142
Venus of Brassempouy, the 129
Venus of Milo 185
Venus sculptures 18
Verch Gwair, Afandreg 248
Vesica Pisces 96, 104
Vessel of the Fish 96
Vesta 119, 161
Victorian Americans 13
village 21, 164
violence 23
Virgil 74, 75, 91, 137, 148
Virgin Mary 16, 36, 40, 42, 96, 104, 106, 111, 119, 121, 137
Virgin-Creatress 139
virgin-mothers 39, 150
Virgin-Mothers of the world 150
vitalistic nature 18
Viviane 58
Voice Of The People Is The Voice Of Goddess, The 145
void 31, 69, 77
votive relief 103
vulva 19, 39, 44, 54, 61, 96, 125-127
vulva-like hills 126
Vut-Imi 90
V's 22
Wah-Kah-Nee 58
Wakahirume 58
Wales 26, 58, 88, 150, 248

walls of houses and caves 19
Waramurungundji 58, 90
Wari-Ma-Te-Takere 151
Washington, George 76
water 58, 59, 67, 79, 175, 179
waves 68
Wawalag Sisters 151
weaponry used for killing other humans 21
Webster's (androcentric) dictionary 40
Wednesday 27
Welsh word 26
Western calender 110
Western monotheistic religions 15
Western scientific materialism 24
Westerners 16, 17, 119
When God was a Woman (Stone) 13
White Buffalo Woman 90
Whom Goddess Wishes To Destroy, She First Makes Mad 147
whore 126
Whore-Goddess 126
Wicce 12
Wiccens 72
wide flaring hips 18
widow 46
Wilden Wip 58
William I 248
Wisdom 10, 122, 124, 159, 168, 171, 173, 182
Witchcraft 12, 167, 174, 175
witches 61, 156, 176
witch-like customs 123
With Goddess' Favor 147
With Goddess' Help 147
Woden 47, 55, 105, 117

Woden's Day 27, 55
Woden-Thor-Saxnot 47
wolves 66
woman   13, 18, 20, 27-29, 39, 43-45, 59, 67, 79, 84, 90, 103, 123, 124,
 146-149, 174, 176, 180, 182, 245
Woman Clothed with the Sun 79
Woman Of Goddess 43, 44, 147
Woman Proposes, Goddess Disposes 148
Woman Upstairs, The 148
womankind 19, 27
woman's house 29
woman's psyche 52
womb of darkness 69
womb of the Great Goddess 96
women . . 2, 3, 10, 12, 15, 18, 20-24, 27, 28, 40, 41, 43, 52, 53, 58, 66,
 84, 85, 95, 110, 114, 115, 148-150, 152, 155, 157-160, 172,
 174, 177, 248
Women's Spirituality Movement 3, 5, 6, 12-14, 16, 30, 40
womyn 114
Word made flesh 72
Word of God 16, 149
Word of Goddess 17, 65, 72, 131, 139, 149, 152, 153
Word Of The Lady, The 152
Word of the Lord 152
Word, the 72
word-power 149
word-title 60, 61, 105
worldwide Lunar Year of Goddess 95
worldwide Religion of Goddess 87
world's Creatresses 87
Wotan 55
Wrath of Goddess, The 153
writing 3, 67, 149, 247

Wudu-Maer	59
W's	22
Xatel-Ekwa	58
Xochiquetzal	58
Yahu	105
Yahweh	64, 66, 76, 87, 105, 117, 123, 124, 152, 155
Yak	58
yawn	64
yawning	64
year of our lady	110, 112
Yebaad	90
Yehowshuwa	105
Yemaya	58, 119
Yemen	124
Yeshua	105
yoni	39, 125
Y's	22
Zaramama	119
Zeus	39, 66, 68, 105, 117, 152
Zima	58
Zion	122
Zodiac	78, 112, 161
Zuni	89, 151
Zywi	58
Zywie	90

"The Creation of Woman," 14th-Century relief on the Cathedral of Orvieto.

Another view of the Cnidian Venus.

The Venus of Panderma, now Bandirma, Turkey.

 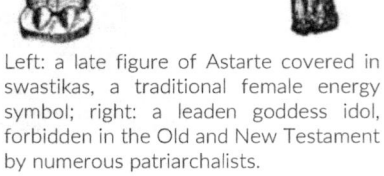

Astarte with a dove on her left arm, a traditional female symbol of love and peace.

Left: a late figure of Astarte covered in swastikas, a traditional female energy symbol; right: a leaden goddess idol, forbidden in the Old and New Testament by numerous patriarchalists.

MEET THE AUTHOR

NEO-VICTORIAN SCHOLAR LOCHLAINN SEABROOK, a descendant of the families of Alexander Hamilton Stephens, John Singleton Mosby, Edmund Winchester Rucker, and William Giles Harding, is a 7th generation Kentuckian and the most prolific pro-South writer in the world today. Known by literary critics as the "new Shelby Foote," the "Southern Joseph Campbell," and the "American Robert Graves," he is a recipient of the prestigious Jefferson Davis Historical Gold Medal. As a lifelong writer he has authored and edited books ranging in topics from history, politics, science, religion, and biography, to nature, music, humor, gastronomy, and the paranormal; books that his readers describe as "game changers," "transformative," and "life altering."

One of the world's most popular living historians, he is a 17th generation Southerner of Appalachian heritage who descends from dozens of patriotic Revolutionary War soldiers and Confederate soldiers from Kentucky, Tennessee, North Carolina, and Virginia. A proud member of the Sons of the Confederate Veterans, he began life as a child prodigy, later transforming into a true Renaissance Man. Besides being an accomplished and well respected author-historian and Bible authority, he is also a Kentucky Colonel, eagle scout, screenwriter, nature, wildlife, and landscape photographer, artist, graphic designer, songwriter (3,000 songs), film composer, multi-instrument musician, vocalist, session player, music producer, genealogist, former history museum docent, and a former ranch hand, zookeeper, and wrangler.

His (currently) 77 adult and children's books contain some 60,000 well-researched pages that have earned him accolades from around the globe. His works, which have sold on every continent except Antarctica, have introduced hundreds of thousands to vital facts that have been left out of our mainstream books. He has been endorsed internationally by leading experts, museum curators, award-winning historians, bestselling authors, celebrities, filmmakers, noted scientists, well regarded educators, TV show hosts and producers, renowned military artists, esteemed heritage organizations, and distinguished academicians of all races, creeds, and colors. Colonel Seabrook holds the world record for writing the most books on Southern icon Nathan Bedford Forrest: 12.

Of northern, western, and central European ancestry, he is the 6th great-grandson of the Earl of Oxford and a descendant of European royalty. His modern day cousins include: Johnny Cash, Elvis Presley, Lisa Marie Presley, Billy Ray and Miley Cyrus, Patty Loveless, Tim McGraw, Lee Ann Womack, Dolly Parton, Pat Boone, Naomi, Wynonna, and Ashley Judd, Ricky Skaggs, the Sunshine Sisters, Martha Carson, Chet Atkins, Patrick J. Buchanan, Cindy Crawford, Bertram Thomas Combs (Kentucky's 50th governor), Edith Bolling (second wife of President Woodrow Wilson), Andy Griffith, Riley Keough, George C. Scott, Robert Duvall, Reese Witherspoon, Lee Marvin, Rebecca Gayheart, and Tom Cruise.

A constitutionalist and avid outdoorsman and gun advocate, Colonel Seabrook is the author of the international blockbuster, *Everything You Were Taught About the Civil War is Wrong, Ask a Southerner!* He lives with his wife and family in beautiful historic Middle Tennessee, the heart of the Confederacy.

For more information on author Mr. Seabrook visit
LochlainnSeabrook.com

Col. Seabrook's Matriarchal Ancestry

Descending from a long line of powerful women and Goddess-worshipers, some of Lochlainn's more notable female ancestors include:

- Queen Boudicca of the ancient Icenians (Lochlainn's 40th great-grandmother).
- Queen Sibyl Fitzseward of Scotland (his 27th great-grandmother).
- Queen Dubhehoblaigh of Ireland (34th great-grandmother).
- Afandreg Verch Gwair Princess of Wales (30th great-grandmother).
- Saint Margaret Atheling Queen of Scotland and England (26th great-grandmother).
- "Lady Godiva" Countess of Mercia (31st great-grandmother).
- Queen Matilda Baldwin of England (26th great-grandmother and the wife of William I the Conqueror).
- Queen Isabella "the Fair" of England (23rd great-grandmother and the wife of Edward II King of England).
- Queen Thyra Danebod of Denmark (32nd great-grandmother).
- Empress Octavia Major Tiberius of Rome (43rd great-grandmother and the wife of Mark Anthony Emperor of Rome).

Beannaich a'bhandia leat

Venus sending out the dove, from a vase.

If you enjoyed Col. Seabrook's *Goddess Dictionary* you will be interested in his other popular related works:

- Seabrook's Bible Dictionary of Traditional & Mystical Doctrines
- Christmas Before Christianity: How the Birthday of the "Sun" Became the Birthday of the "Son"
- Britannia Rules: Goddess-Worship in Ancient Anglo-Celtic Society
- The Book of Kelle: An Introduction to Goddess-Worship & the Great Celtic Mother-Goddess Kelle
- Jesus & the Gospel of Q: Christ's Pre-Christian Teachings as Recorded in the New Testament
- Christ Is All & In All: Rediscovering Your Divine Nature & the Kingdom Within
- Jesus & the Law of Attraction: The Bible-Based Guide to Creating Perfect Health, Wealth, & Happiness
- The Bible & the Law of Attraction: 99 Teachings of Jesus, the Apostles & the Prophets

Available from Sea Raven Press and wherever fine books are sold.

ALL OF OUR BOOK COVERS ARE AVAILABLE AS 11" X 17" POSTERS, SUITABLE FOR FRAMING.

SeaRavenPress.com

www.ingramcontent.com/pod-product-compliance
Lightning Source LLC
Chambersburg PA
CBHW032222080426
42735CB00008B/680